W9-AUU-921

Date: 6/1/20

BIO MORAGA
Moraga, Cherríe,
Native country of the heart :
a memoir /

NATIVE COUNTRY
OF THE HEART

NATIVE COUNTRY OF THE HEART

A MEMOIR

CHERRÍE MORAGA

FARRAR, STRAUS AND GIROUX

NEW YORK

Farrar, Straus and Giroux
175 Varick Street, New York 10014

Printed in the United States of America
First edition, 2019

Library of Congress Cataloging-in-Publication Data
Names: Moraga, Cherríe, author.
Title: Native country of the heart : a memoir / Cherríe Moraga.
Description: First edition. | New York : Farrar, Straus and Giroux, 2019. |
    Includes bibliographical references.
Identifiers: LCCN 2018041574 | ISBN 9780374219666 (hardcover)
Subjects: LCSH: Moraga, Cherríe—Family. | Mexican American women
    authors—Biography.
Classification: LCC PS3563.O753 Z46 2019 | DDC 818/.5409 [B]—dc23
LC record available at https://lccn.loc.gov/2018041574

Designed by Abby Kagan

Our books may be purchased in bulk for promotional, educational, or business
    use. Please contact your local bookseller or the Macmillan Corporate and
Premium Sales Department at 1-800-221-7945, extension 5442, or by e-mail at
    MacmillanSpecialMarkets@macmillan.com.

www.fsgbooks.com
www.twitter.com/fsgbooks • www.facebook.com/fsgbooks

1 3 5 7 9 10 8 6 4 2

For my sister, JoAnn.
And for our ancestors.

CONTENTS

AUTHOR'S NOTE

ON NAMING
Some people's names in this memoir were changed or were replaced with generic identifiers.

ON LANGUAGE
The Spanish in this work emerged when the writing naturally evoked it. Not that much, but enough, I hope, for the reader to experience this writing as a *Mexican*American work.

There came a time in my life when I began to look backwards, like those mixed-race figures depicted in eighteenth-century Mexican Casta paintings. In the portrait where I imagine myself, I am "una salta pa'tras," a "throwback" mixed-blood child. She sits upon the white father's lap and twists her head almost violently backwards to gaze upon the countenance and the continent of the Indian mother.

—C.M.

NATIVE COUNTRY
OF THE HEART

PROLOGUE—UNA SALTA PA'TRAS

Elvira Isabel Moraga was not the stuff of literature. Few bemoan the memory loss of the unlettered. My mother—and her generation of MexicanAmerican women—was to disappear quietly, unmarked by the letter of memory, the memory of letter. But when our storytellers go, taking their unrecorded memory with them, we their descendants go too, I fear.

Maybe it's about turning sixty. Maybe at such a substantive age, one can finally weave together enough of the threads of one's life to interpret a design from them. For my part, I hold one thickly braided cord as story—my queer self and my writer self, and each would bring me home to my Mexicanism. And my Mexicanism would bring me home to an earlier América; to the Indian memory of bay leaf and madrone, desert chaparral, the Pacific always an ocean breeze away. It would also bring home to me a culture of memory and prophesy—the harbinger of loss upon the horizon.

As a U.S. inheritor of Mexican ancestry, I have walked the reddening road of an "Occupied America" that anoints membership only to those born north of the watery divide of el Río Grande. A border of river as thirsty as the desert into which it bleeds, leaving my relatives to drown in its grit. Growing up, my elders, well-meaning, told my generation—*Go that way, hijos. Look north to your future.* They asked us to betray them, to forget them.

Walk that way, mi' ja.

They didn't know the cost.

How to explain the complexity of this? What it means to be— not just *me* but *us*. To know yourself as a member of a pueblo on the edge of a kind of extinction, and at the same time a lesbian lover and mother, where you truly do live your life in constant navigation through whatever part of your identity is being snuffed out that morning—in the classroom, at the community meeting, the gasoline station, the take-out counter—Mexican, mixed-blood, queer, female, almost-Indian. And a poverty masked by circumstance.

For all my feminism, this is why I left a white women's movement in the late 1970s. So I wouldn't have to explain anymore, translate anymore. Because translating, I knew, would keep me from the harder work of going home: of trying to figure out, within the context of my ethnicity and culture, what Mexican & American / Indian & Catholic / rape & racism had to do with sexual desire and a contrary gender. And, just maybe, my return as a writer would matter to my pueblo. Maybe, in some small way, my visible queerness—which I knew was representative of so many others—could help make us a more resilient people.

Perhaps my writing has never really been about me. Perhaps it was about *she* all along: *she* without letters; *she* fallen off the map of recorded histories; *she* that is my history and my future with every mexicana female worker who comes to, or is born into, these lands of an ill-manifested destiny. *She*, the first and last point of my return.

There was no library in our home growing up. I did not sneak to read beneath the secrecy of flashlights under blankets. My reading stumbled out loud and my handwriting fell thick and crooked on wide-ruled paper. But I knew to listen. I listened to Elvira's stories, to my tías' stories, to my sister's promptings, "Remember this moment, hermanita." I made mental records of their words, of being read to at night by that same sister who believed in romance, something that came on a horse and swept a woman up, not so unlike Elvira's dreams.

I had only one romance—the love of an intractable Elvira, and this is what would shape my lesbianism and this is what would mark my road as a Mexican and this is what would require me to remember before and beyond my mother. I am a woman who knew myself daughter and son at once—a protector and provider for women and children. I have learned to confront police and rapists and silent enemies from within and have lived to tell of it.

I had never fully grasped the early years of my mother's life until I slowed down long enough to silently witness her last ones. In her final handful of years, the full distance of a near-century lifetime would flash back in a second of recall, never to reappear. And yet my mother's failing mind once and forever convinced me of the body's ability to hold memory, which long surpassed her ability to speak it. It seems that when the body goes, memory resides in the molecules about us. We breathe in the last exhale of our mothers' breath. This is what they bequeath to us. As they also bequeath their stories.

Elvira's is the story of our forgotten, the landscape of loss paved over by American dreams come true. And maybe that's the worst of it (or what I fear)—that our dreams *can* come true in "America," but at the cost of a profound senility of spirit. *If we forget ourselves, who will be left to remember us?*

And so I followed the trail of my mother's fleeting reminiscences, picking up in the wake of her steps each and every discarded scrap of unwritten testimonio. This is what the spiritual country of my mother's departure asked of me, in the unspoken world of the deeply human.

PART I

COYOTE'S DAUGHTER

My mother, in her little black sweater with the faux fur collar and fake string of pearls, is celebrating her ninetieth birthday. Seeing her made-up like this, even amid the obligatory pleasantly pastel decor of twenty-first-century eldercare suburbia, I catch a momentary glimpse of Elvira's past, she who appeared in the sepia-toned photographs of a late-1920s "Golden Age" Tijuana: Elvirita, linking arms with her girlfriends in front of the Foreign Club; sprawled beneath the bare arm of a fledgling city tree; hip to hip with her cuate, Esperanza, on the bumper of a Model A Ford. Elvira: in the calf-length shapely skirt, the matching white heels, and the low-slung blouse with its draping bow. The bright red lips that do not smile, but invite, as is appropriate for the era. Elvira had a grand life before her children ever came into it.

There were no fathers in the Moraga clan, not in those first Aztlán turn-into-the-twenty-first-century generations. There were men, yes; men who came and left the household with a single man's prerogative and secrets; men who answered to no one, and never to a female.

It is 1925. Elvirita is eleven years old. She is picking cotton in the Imperial Valley, just north of the California-Mexico border. Her father is the freelance contractor for the job. He has hired out his school-aged unmarried children (what remain of the nine) to work the fields. Elvira wears one sack draped over the square bone of her thin shoulder. As she stuffs it full of cotton balls, she drags another sack, laden with the three-year-old weight of her littlest brother, Eduardito.

My mother cried the first time she told me this story. I was a little girl and I cried, too, at the picture of it. A picture of hardship, yes; but more than that—injustice. For most of her childhood in California, my mother's father regularly pulled his children out of school and bartered them out to labor in the fields. She never said the word *profit*—that the fewer laborers he contracted outside of la familia, the more money would end up in his personal pocket. As I left the kitchen of my mother's stories, I came to understand that her sense of injustice was not so much that she and her young siblings had to work in the fields. Many of my Chicano and Chicana counterparts knew farmwork as a regular occurrence growing up, their school schedules shaved off at both ends to accommodate the seasons. And although, of course, child labor in a just world would be outlawed, within a U.S.-Mexican context where poverty *is* law, child labor was common practice. It was the *intimacy* of the injustice that seemed to wound my mother the most; that although the near-dozen Moragas struggled economically, she believed my grandfather had a choice in the matter.

Born on the U.S. side of the border, they had also always lived on the other side of the (Mexican) tracks (or so my mother made a point of saying). She also insisted that when she was a girl her family never sat in the Mexican section of the movie house. "We were a difernt claz of peepo," referring to herself and her eight Spanish-speaking siblings. Years of migrant farm labor did not, in my mother's mind, bind them economically (or culturally) to the rest of the Mexican immigrant population. Or so she protested against an immutable and unspoken identification with them.

For most of my childhood, my mother hid the truth of her father's drunkenness and outlaw scams: Moraga the bootlegger, Moraga the labor contractor, Moraga the human smuggler. Like el coyote, that illusive trickster who shuttles between worlds, Esteban Moraga rode the counterfeit borders of the Southwest with a vaquero flair of Mexican independence and macho bravado. Yeah, it was a Wild West life, but at its heart Elvira remained a naïve and tender teenaged girl relinquishing her wages and tips to buy the carne for the caldo, the harina for the tortillas, la manteca para los frijoles. This was the political economy my mother had known since childhood and that would continue as the Depression hit and Esteban Moraga moved the familia south to Tijuana's "Golden Age of Vice."

My mother would never return to school after that. It had already become too embarrassing: a girl of eleven stuck into classrooms with third graders. "The last time I was in school, I was so big, the teacher would step out and leave me in charge half the time." My mother's bitterness (or better said, shame) about her lack of formal education was tacitly evident in every palsied signature she applied to grocery store checks, every job application my sister and I helped her complete, every school notice we brought home to sit abandoned and unread on the kitchen table.

Her inability to read and write well remained an open wound for Elvira her entire life, as she believed it was the single thing that separated her from that coveted *other* life of an office job where women wore skirts and stockings to work each day, and used their minds instead of their hands to bring home a paycheck. Despite that belief, Elvira's full decade of employment in 1930s Tijuana was to provide her with an education far beyond the confines of the labor camp and the schoolyard.

In 1929, as white men were taking nosedives off skyscrapers on Wall Street and Prohibition was in full swing, "Border Baron" Wirt Bowman was making a handsome profit six miles south of the border through his investment in the casino and racetrack business, notably the Agua Caliente and the Foreign Club. While Dust Bowl survivors blew into the agricultural fields of California, two million Mexicans (including Mexican*Americans*) were "repatriated" to México to make room for them. But the Moraga clan was not among the families herded onto boxcars, without regard to citizenship, in Los Angeles, Chicago, and San Francisco. Theirs was a voluntary exodus, inspired by rising anti-Mexican sentiment and joblessness in Alta California, while Baja California witnessed a swelling American-financed industry of gambling and prostitution afloat in a Pacific Ocean of unrestricted liquor.

"Cigarettes, candy, chewing gum."

Amid spinning roulette wheels and the red and black flashes of diamonds and spades, a petite five-feet-one-inch fourteen-year-old Elvira stands a few inches taller in first-time high heels teetering over her sales tray of the icons of American advertising: Camel, Lucky Strike, and Chesterfield cigarettes; Hershey's and Milky Way candy bars; Chiclets, Juicy Fruit, and Wrigley's Spearmint gum. Lying about her age with a fairly fluid bilingualism, she wrangled a job as a cigarette and hatcheck girl at the coveted Salón de Oro at the Agua Caliente, a high-stakes gambling room frequented by Hollywood's finest. Elvira would remain in its employ until President Lázaro Cárdenas outlawed casinos in 1935.

"Check your hats and coats here, please."

I often wondered if my mother's years in the Salón de Oro had ruined her—made an ordinary Mexican life in the United States impossible; made her relationship to Gringolandia an ever-promise that would betray her. *How you gonna keep 'em down on the farm after they've seen Tijuana in the '30s?*

At Agua Caliente, Elvira glimpsed a world that was dream years away from the home of makeshift tents they had posted in the melon fields of Imperial Valley just months before. In Tijuana, Elvira literally touched hands with movie stars—Gary Cooper, Clark Gable, Jean Harlow—and Mafia bosses, Al Capone included, as they dropped silver dollars into her open palm. The tips spilled into her pockets like jackpot winnings. Then after her shift, returning home at four o'clock in the morning, she would deposit all her earnings into the open coffer of her mother's expectant hands.

"I never thought to keep any of it for myself. I bought my clothes for work, but all the rest was for them. Maybe that was stupid of me. I was just a girl."

Elvira was loath to tell that as she made her way home a few hours before dawn each night, she often encountered her father headed along the same path, stumbling with a belly full of drink, at times his face in a ditch vomiting. "I would just take another street home," she told me. "I hated to see him like that."

My mother's silence around her father was unlike her invocation to another man, whose name fell from her lips with a kind of hallowed reverence. It bothered me, how her voice would change when she spoke of "Mr. Bowman" all those years later. A slightly affected tone, almost flirtatious. There was a lie in it somehow; it hinted of something unreconciled, undone.

Wirt Bowman, as a major owner of Agua Caliente, appeared

in my mother's Tijuana stories as a faceless benefactor. Although he died in 1949, one year into my mother's marriage to my father, Bowman seemed to hold a part of Elvira's history hostage. I never knew his first name, never asked her, only looked it up years later when it occurred to me that the man might've been some kind of real big shot in his time.

I first found his name mentioned in a thin paperback I was never able to find again. Years later, however, at a used bookstore in L.A. I landed upon a title, *Pozo del Mundo*, a book copyrighted in 1970 that depicts Tijuana and the world of the Mexican-American border, employing every stereotype of Mexican low-life debauchery ever invented by the gringo imagination. The book also contains several pages on Bowman and his many incarnations as cattleman, bootlegger, gunrunner during the Mexican revolution (for profit, not politics), casino owner, and, after Mexican gambling was outlawed, an Arizona statesman (predictably).

To us, growing up, he was just "Mr. Bowman," who had featured in my mother's life as a kind of silent patron. *Patrón*, as it is understood in Spanish, may be more apropos; for, first and foremost, Bowman was my mother's boss. Still, there were the unaccounted-for benefits. "He paid for my father's funeral," she told me. "He didn't have to do that." Like he didn't have to give her a full month's paid leave to recover from a bronchitis they had feared was tuberculosis, which had left her on the verge of collapse and her family without any means of support. "I don't know what we would've done without him," she said, almost contrite.

Even before her father's death from pneumonia in 1934, Elvira was the financial mainstay of the family of eight still living at home. By the late 1920s, since the older sisters, Dolores, Victoria, and Hortensia, had all married in their teens, Elvira shouldered the bulk of the family financial burden, along with a reluctant Josefina, a few years younger. Her older brother, Esteban, was the missing link in the chain of family responsibilities. "He was a very good-looking man" was the parenthetical spliced between the mostly nonstory told about his work life, his love life, his family life.

One time, at her mother's urging, Elvira asked Bowman to give Esteban Jr. a job interview. "I had bought him a new suit. Shoes, a hat, the works," my mother recounts the event I had already memorized. But I love her telling of it. She describes the quality fabric of the suit; how my uncle's broad shoulders filled it with an actor's elegance. The brim of his hat bent over the intelligent brow and warm mouth. It is what my mother always did best—to own a piece of a man in that way, in the way we women so often prop them up for the visuals, the look of someone who *could* be a man, a provider, someone you can count on.

"Aren't you ashamed," Bowman asked him in their meeting, hiring him on the spot, "that your little sister has to do this for you? What kind of man are you?" Her brother's response was to keep the "drapes" and head for the cantina, never appearing for a day's work.

But Bowman was no saint. I knew from the sheer math of it that he was close to sixty as he bestowed his kindnesses upon the teenaged Elvira; and that, as she grew older, her required sexual submission would come to be a simple matter of payback. He would twice try to arrange a sexual liaison with her, for which fate and faith dictated a different outcome. I sensed there was some guilt in this for my mother (because she did believe she owed him), mixed with an insistent pride that she had slipped from his imperious grasp. Malinche she was not.

I lie.

Of course Elvira was Malinche. Malintzín Tenepal, our sixteenth-century Indigenous mother, sold into slavery by her own relations, transported from the Nahuatl language of her origins to the Mayan of her esclavitud. There among the Tabascans embattled by the Spanish, on the southern edge of the gulf waters, she is presented to El Conquistador, Hernán Cortés, in a gesture of reconciliation.

As Malinche shows prowess in multiple tongues, Cortés takes her as his concubine and interpreter. And with her as strategic guide at his side, the conquest of Indigenous México is realized.

Or so the story goes.

The figure of Malinche wrestles inside the collective unconscious of every Mexican female. She murmurs in a distant indiscernible voice that the official story is not the whole story; that Malinche was not free and was proffered freedom for her services. We hear the devil temptation in the tale; that our sex is our sin and our salvation; that it can be used, along with our wits and wiles, to save ourselves, our families, and our people; that there are mouths to feed and men who are not doing their share for their own good reasons.

Maybe those reasons are historical disappointments, the cultural memory of themselves as once Aztec royalty or Spanish rancheros. *I deserve better than this, the Mexican man senses somewhere in his DNA and maybe he resents his wife, who wears a little brighter skin, a little more Spanish entitlement or at least the "airs" to suggest it, and so the father drinks and the sons drink after him and they hustle the gringo in the best way they can, güey, because they remember better days, days better than the white man (so inferior in looks and intelligence) running the joint, the construction company, the downtown restaurant, the stock exchange, and the whole pinche Rancho del Norte.*

Beneath this grand sweep of history resides the small whispered story of a woman. In this story, the Mexican man uses his daughter to do the stepping and the fetching. He sells her out to do his bidding. And he remains uncompromised. In this story, Elvira is sold over and over like Malinche was sold into slavery and a life of treachery. And like Malinche, Elvira marvels at her destiny, that she, somehow, is not one of the two million Mexicans put into boxcars and returned to a life of poverty. Instead, she walks south across the border as the stock market crashes behind her. And, like the Indian Malinche, she learns to talk out of both sides of her mouth. *They made me a slave and condemn me when I act like one.* This split tongue was my mother's language, as she negotiated the advances of her own Cortés in the person of Wirt Bowman.

In the early 1930s, Rosarito Beach is a short day trip down the coast from Tijuana. My mother is now eighteen years old and has been working for Bowman for nearly four years. He invites her to accompany him to the famous, newly renovated resort Hotel Rosarito. The limousine, driven by Felipe, the chauffeur, arrives to pick her up. Bowman is in the back seat. Felipe, a friend and co-worker of Elvira's, averts his eyes as he opens the door to let her in. This ritual of propriety that attempts to mask the unspoken intent of the excursion embarrasses them equally. Felipe and she both know that she is neither Bowman's wife nor his daughter. The Rosarito Beach Hotel, which movie stars and Mexican dignitaries frequent, does not proffer entrada to an unmarried Mexican girl without a maid's wash bin or her patrón's elbow. She knows how she will be viewed as she crosses under the Moorish archways of the hotel.

As the car door slams behind her, Bowman slaps the leather seat, a summons for Elvira to slide over next to him. She does. He does not touch her, except paternally, but Elvira knows what is up ahead at the end of the dusty road. This is not how she imagined it. Todavía una señorita, she would be ruined after this, but is utterly unable to say no. Her family depends upon her. So Elvira did the only thing she knew to do, she prayed and prayed and prayed toward the god of that endless ocean, steady and insistent outside her window, responding to Bowman's idle conversation in murmured monosyllables.

Until without warning, the car begins to lurch and spit and slowly sputters to a dead stop.

"Señor Bowman," the chauffeur also sputters, "I don't know what's wrong. I promise you, I filled the tank just before leaving."

The bone-dry tank was testimony to my mother's faith in God, or this is how she told the story to us as little girls. I was so little in those earliest tellings, I remember not quite knowing what it was that Mr. Bowman wanted from my mother. I came to understand this more fully later, along with suspecting it was not a "miracle" but the chauffeur who had purposely underfilled the gas tank for my mother's sake.

Or . . . maybe not.

"What god are you praying to?" was all Bowman had to say to my mother. And with that el patrón himself ran out of gas against the protest of my mother's prayers.

Several years later, in the 1940s, Bowman would make one last effort to collect on his generosity. After the newly elected President Cárdenas had closed down the casinos in Tijuana, my mother stayed on for a spell at the Foreign Club, selling perfumes. By 1939, she and the family had returned to Los Angeles, and within a year her elder brother would be dead. My mother describes the barroom brawl, the heavy metal napkin holder flying across the room and landing on the side of Esteban's face. "He wasn't part of the fight," she insists. "He was just on his way to the bathroom." Esteban would die of lockjaw from the infected wound.

Fatherless and now without her elder brother's presence, Elvira remained tethered to her mother's incessant demands, serving as second mother to her two youngest siblings while serving as breadwinner and tortilla maker to all. Her younger brother, Roberto, barely eighteen, was busing tables at the Biltmore Hotel, through a connection Elvira had with Bowman and Bowman had with the Biltmore.

Almost twenty-five years old and Elvira is without a husband, reciting silently to herself a troubled litany of Mexican suitors on both sides of the border—one who turned up with a wife, another with unmentioned children or more insidious secrets. There were serenades and marriage proposals that would not stick. Meanwhile, her middle-aged mother, who had been married since the age of fourteen, seeks out a love life of her own.

Elvira receives notice from Bowman, who summons her to appear at the bar of the Biltmore, where he is staying. She arrives, dressed to the nines. She knows he will want her, but the dress-up is not meant to entice him. Instead she intends to reflect that she is holding herself up with some "class," my mother's word for dignity.

She describes the melting drink between them, the perspiration rising on her forehead. Her hands cling to the pocketbook on her lap. He is slightly irritated by Elvira's obvious nervousness, her body in a fever of fear. He tries not to show it, as he wants to remind her through his composure that he is entitled. Suddenly the moment is interrupted. The waiter approaches apologetically, bringing the heavy metal phone, with its long cord-tail, to the table. The conversation takes less than a minute. Bowman has to leave right away. There are no apologies on his part, but as she watches his back exiting, Elvira whispers aloud, "God forgive me."

There *is* another way to tell my mother's story. It is an Indian story of the encounter between Europe and Native America, between man and woman. In it resides the heartbeat of an abiding contradiction, a compromise my family, like millions of families of MexicanAmerica, has made with AngloAmerica. We do not speak of it, but this is what we know: that we were here first and forever; that our Native origins matter at a profoundly unspoken site of knowing. We know this, even as our feigned collective denial continues to wind itself into the twisted knot of a perjured history, rooted in the same soil as the severed hands, burnt corpses, violated female bodies of the Spanish invasion, and of all the conquests of flesh and spirit that succeeded it.

I come from a long line of vendidas. I inscribe these words as an act of Chicana feminist reclamation, naming the women in my familia traitors within an impossible patriarchy.

SOMETHING BETTER

We began as a mixed-race family of five, Joseph and Vera (as Elvira was called in English) and we three stepladder siblings—James, JoAnn, and I—born within a span of four years in that boom of babies following World War II. In the early 1950s, South Pasadena was at first glance as close as you could get to a Norman Rockwell *Saturday Evening Post* cover. As children, we would leaf through the magazine's pictures on our occasional visits to the family doctor. That we *had* a family doctor, given my father's meager wages, who also made home visits, carrying his small black medicine bag, speaks to the Midwest-movie-set feel of the town. We also had a milkman and an egg man, delivering fresh each week. For us kids, the place was pure Technicolor, a curious confluence of cultures and economic classes that stood about seven miles north of los barrios of East L.A. and the rest of la familia on the south side.

My father operated the town's one-man Santa Fe Railroad station, which stood two short blocks from our house. Within the decade, Santa Fe would witness the retirement of the steam engine locomotive. On the occasion of the engine's historic last stop at the station, we three kids posed for a photo in front of the daunting old *Chief*, as it was called, dwarfed by its black immensity. The *Chief* was soon to be replaced by its offspring, the diesel locomotive. Painted in New Mexican burnt orange and yellow, the Zia Pueblo sun symbol announced the *Super Chief*'s entrance into the Southwest of the 1960s. Many years later, I would come to think of the naming as a perverse requiem for the wholesale slaughter of the buffalo effected by the railroad a hundred years earlier in Indian country.

As our father studied train schedules just down the street, our "stay-at-home mother" took in baskets of ironing and babies full of need to supplement the family's modest income. Elvira was a miracle worker with the babies. She could lay hands on a child and cure him of virtually any malaise, if given enough time. I remember the far-too-skinny white lady bringing her towheaded baby to us. He gazed sleepily through red-rimmed swollen eyes. When my mother pulled back the thin blanket, I heard her suck in her breath at the sight of the drum-hard extended belly, its navel protruding, close to bursting. The baby was old enough to walk but was too weak. There was something wrong with the woman, too. She trembled as she dropped the infant into my mother's arms. That the woman was to blame for the baby's illness I could tell from our mother's cold way with her. She judged her, couldn't understand how someone could let a child starve like that. The baby just needed "love," our mother said when we asked.

So Elvira gave the child love, feeding it to him in tiny teaspoon-size servings like a small bird, until gradually the swollen stomach shrank and I came home from school one day to find the baby standing, grabbing on to the bars of the playpen, like a happy miracle.

Most of what I remember about South Pasadena in those

early years was "happy." You wouldn't know it, though, for all my mother's complaints: about a husband who never understood the function of a screwdriver, a spark plug, a pint of paint, or a lawn mower. I remember that my mother's rantings at our father (and at us) were so constant that Kenny Duncan, our neighbor (who looked like a Mexican but didn't know a word of Spanish), would always laugh knowingly when we'd go over to his house to get out of our mother's hair. "Same old jazz, Momma!" he used to chant every time we appeared at his back door, begging entrance.

"We're Indian," his eldest, Linda, introduced herself with a kind of defensive pride. "Sioux," she announced, "on our dad's side." And since our mom was Mexican, we were pretty much on the same side. Linda's mother was lazy and white and too fat (my mother's opinion) for the ruggedly handsome Mr. Duncan, a plumber and "a man who worked with his hands," which my mother of course admired. I used to think about how much better a couple Mr. Duncan and my mom would've made; he always caring for their front yard, trimming and watering the dichondra, while his wife stayed indoors, reading women's magazines after work. They owned and we rented; that was one difference, but the other one was my father's utter lack of interest in physical labor of any kind. Sometimes, Mr. Duncan would feel so sorry for my mom, who always kept herself as lean and manicured as his dichondra, that he'd come over and mow our front yard bristling with raggedy crabgrass.

"Doesn't it make you ashamed?" my mom would ask my dad. His silence always answered the question.

My mother's at-home childcare enterprise forged deep relationships with single working mothers and their children that would last for decades. Norma Delgado equaled my mom in good looks and work ethic and in their whispered histories of handsome and faithless suitors. I remember the two of them in the late afternoon, cigarette raised in one hand, coffee cup at their fingertips in the other, laughing in a seamless Spanglish that dotted my imagination. Between the intervals of words I recognized and those I did not, full stories were hidden. In the years to come, holding court among the tías in her afternoon kitchen, Elvira would never tell all, but what she did tell affected a moral rectitude that kept us niñas rooted to the drama, piecing together the plotline between languages.

Norma's daughter Cecilia was older, thick-limbed and a deep café brown in contrast to her baby sister, la güerita. The baby sister was of little interest to me, but Cecilia was full of fun and early teen knowledge. As she lifted me up onto my gift of her hand-me-down Schwinn, we were both disappointed to discover that my feet couldn't quite reach the pedals. So, not to be dissuaded, she held the bike strong, as I fixed my unsteady feet onto the pedals, and with one great shove, Cecilia sent me off down Meridian Street, me standing upright and pedaling furiously all the way around the block and back again.

Of all the children my mother cared for, I remember little Paul the most clearly: he, standing in the playpen, his thick black Navajo hair poking straight up from his head, his eager smile—so wide it dug arrowheads into the twin mounds of his cafecito-colored cheeks. I felt Paul as my own little brother, taking that kind of care with him, helping my mom feed him and chasing after him as he learned to walk. His mother, Vee, eventually lost her mixed-blood husband and children to her love of alcohol. I remember my mother's rejection of her, years later, after the divorce, when she came to visit my parents in our home in San Gabriel.

"Give me a drink, Joe," Vee hollered at my father, barely a foot into the door and plopping down on the couch. This was how my mother described it. Elvira's thick contempt for those she once loved who had disappointed her distanced my mother from the heartbreak of it. In my mother's relationships, she offered good counsel that might be rejected once, twice, maybe even a third time; but after that it was over.

Vee would not be fixed.

I remember Vee's deep brown eyes, her round chata face, and what I heard as a slight swallowing of her syllables that I came to understand later as a Dineh inflection. There was so much I came to understand *later*, how the broad planes of Kenny Duncan's face were sculpted with the same engravings I saw upon the faces of the Lakota; that the small twig of his aged and silent mother held a place in history, which located the modern-day Kenny, his look-alike brother, and their crazy ever-partying little sister, Peggy, in a longed-for landscape of post–World War II American entitlement. Hadn't they earned inclusion? For their generation of urban Indian, what use was there in remembering? But by 1969, there was the American Indian Movement and the occupation of Alcatraz and the 1973 siege at Wounded Knee that would not forget.

In the decade following, my almost-little-brother, Paul, would grow up to be a doctor, doing his residency on his mother's rez in Arizona. Several years later, Vee's youngest son would come by to see my mom, like so many of her friend's children eventually did. I was there on a visit when he walked into my mother's kitchen—a veritable Hollywood Indian beauty, tall and lean and hungry—and that's where he was headed: to Hollywood.

"Figure I can find work there," he said. He had just come by to get my mother's blessing. And, no doubt, a taco or two of her steak picado.

Looking back to that first decade after World War II, which everyone wanted to believe was the "good war," the three and a half square miles of South Pasadena served as a kind of suburban holding zone with all manner of people arriving into Greater Los Angeles at the prospect of a 1950s culture of optimism. Still, even in my child's mind there was an "us and them" in the world we occupied, which drew a line between Mexican and gringo culture (my father notwithstanding). Mexican could mean pretty much anyone brown or sort of brown or somehow "foreign" in an English-speaking world. It didn't mean Black. Black was "American" and had its own relationship to "them" (white people), which, as a child, I hardly understood. Until the Civil Rights movement exposed the horror of that relationship; until Black Power shoved it righteously into our faces and Black people became the very measure of injustice and equal rights in this country.

What I remember most about South Pasadena of that period were the parties where all the Moraga relatives came to visit and drank and danced and drank some more and we kids were lined up like sardines in double beds while the grown-ups partied into the night. This was a *Mexican*American life, just like the life of those striving Indians and Black folk, of World War II vets and their pregnant wives with steady work and hopes, finally, of something better.

Before I knew a word of race relations, I knew the images of "colored women" on our small black-and-white TV. I was especially drawn to those "tragic mulatta" stories that struck me as kind of like me. And those dark-haired passing-for-white ladies who suffered the secret of their race in silence didn't really look too different on the TV screen from my mestiza mom, dressed to the nines and mixing cocktails for the party.

LITTLE RASCALS

The Shoemaker was the first Jew I ever met, before I knew anything of the history or cultures of Jews. I was five years old. The Shoemaker had a thick accent from a very faraway place and his entire shop was wallpapered with red- and black-inked newspaper clippings with markings I later realized were Yiddish. We all liked the old man right away, and his shop smelled like the olden days of shoe polish and tooled leather. He seemed to like us, too, or maybe it was mostly our mom he liked when he told her that we kids were different from the rowdy gringo ones that hung around the tracks near his shop and treated him like a stranger.

The railroad tracks cut diagonally through our neighborhood and served as the shortcut and meeting ground for our motley crew of mixed-blood/mixed-size kids. There, sitting on the tracks in an act of defiance against the distant rumbling of an approaching train, my sister and I would eat our hot-off-the-comal buttered tortillas de harina freshly rolled inside our palms.

"What are you eating?" the white boy asked. "Yeah, it looks like burned paper," the other goaded.

"They are tortillas," we answered, appalled by their ignorance.

I never thought about whether the Shoemaker had a wife or children or grandkids. I do know he was a man of passion and it was plastered in bleeding red and bold black on the walls of that small cobbler shop in that not-so-WASP Norman Rockwell town. My dad told me many years later that the establishment of that town "never really approved" of the Shoemaker's presence there. The newspapers were "Communist," he confided with a hint of danger . . . and admiration. I didn't know exactly how that disapproval was expressed. Perhaps it was no harsher than bits of idle gossip, to which my father, alone, was privy as someone who was read simply as a white Protestant, no hint of the Mexican wife at home.

Not until the occasion of my father's ninetieth birthday would he reveal to me that the founding documents of the Exchange Club, to which he had belonged as the local train station manager, restricted membership to whites only. My FDR Democrat father claimed he had no knowledge of this until his resignation from the club, which occurred not in protest but because our family moved to the nearby town of San Gabriel. My father admitted: "I remember there had been an issue with the wife of one of the club members. Seems she had a problem with Vera being Mexican."

"It is often the women," my dad opined.

We three kids would regularly stop in on the Shoemaker and offer him a few tunes like "Que Será, Será" or "You Are My Sunshine." Our repertoire was limited, but he'd pass us some pennies for our efforts. Each time, of course, we had to act like we didn't want or expect the money (good home training), but no sooner had the coins landed in our sweaty summer palms than we'd race across the street to the market to buy some Tootsie Rolls or red braids of rubbery licorice.

James had a beautiful voice, and one of the Shoemaker's favorites was our rendition of "Tom Dooley," with our brother in the lead. A Kingston Trio hit recorded in 1958, this song was a kind of corrido in English with origins in the American South about a guy who ends up killing his woman on a mountain and knows he will be hanged for it.

> *Hang down your head, Tom Doo-oo-leey—*
> *Hang down your head and cry.*

Hardly the repertoire for schoolchildren, but we'd sing con puro gusto, adding little movements that prefigured the Temptations. I was given a special "tomboy" segue, linking the verses, belting out my "ah well-ah now boy," with my index fingers drawn like two six-shooter pistols. We sang often as children, especially with our mom, though her vocal cords had been damaged as a child. It was a freak accident, as she described it. Something about her brother Esteban driving back into camp in the middle of the night, drunk no doubt, and the Model T brake not holding.

Some of my best memories were of us kids singing with our mom. Taking the Pasadena Freeway home from Adams Street, after visiting our grandmother and Uncle Bobby and Auntie Tencha at El Taxco, a small Mexican restaurant they ran in South Los Angeles. Or perhaps we splurged and took the short drive down on the same freeway that dropped you right smack onto Broadway and into the heart of Chinatown. In the central plaza, a real organ grinder played tunes as a small fidgety monkey with a silly cap, just like in *The Little Rascals*, snatched a penny from our outstretched fingers. I remember giggling nervously at the animal touch of the spindly fingers. At the Wishing Well, we fed coins to the Buddhist-style shrine with a waterfall running down its face. Standing on our tiptoes, we tossed pennies toward the little bronze bowls marked "Prosperity," "Fortune," "Peace," "Love," or a custom-designed "Your Wish."

Suddenly sleepy from the MSG in the Chinese Dinner #2, we'd make our way home, speeding through the three cement tunnels carved through the rocky canyon of Chavez Ravine. As we approached each tunnel, one after the other, we'd let out our breath with an extended "Aaaaaaaaah" to see whose could last the longest.

Then it was our usual Shoemaker repertoire of songs to get us the rest of the way home, my dad sometimes chiming in from the driver's seat, his voice enthusiastic, but utterly off-key. We'd hold our ears—"No, Daddy, please don't"—laughing. And gradually, we'd hear my mother's voice start to go hoarse and this was the cue for we three kids to kick in with our closing number.

"Put your arms around me, honey, hold me tight."

Our mom had taught us kids all the hand gestures, hugging our bodies as we "huddled up and cuddled up with all [our] might." Rolling our eyes at each other with the line "eyes that I just idolize." Our bodies "rockin' like a motorboat" to the beat of our love-struck hearts. All this leading up to the grand finale, where we sang full throttle—

"Oooooh, babe, I never knew such a ga-a-a-a-al . . . li-i-i-i-ke . . ."

Pointing to our mom, all three in unison. "You-ou-ou-ou!"

She always acted surprised, like she was the last person she expected us to point to!

I got my wish every time.

WHAT EVER HAPPENED TO
NORMAN ROCKWELL?

Bleach-blond high-heeled Hallie Huff, my father's mother, was in her fifties when in 1940 she gave up her San Francisco stage actress career on a gamble. Urged by her sister, she moved south to manage, and in time was able to buy, a second-class second-story hotel in the oil-derrick-dotted town of Huntington Beach, California. Soon World War II broke out, followed by Korea, and the Kenwood Hotel would bring in a sea of soldiers and a flow of cash.

Grandma Hallie's two-bedroom manager's apartment was "exotic" long before I could make sense of the word. The living room, which looked over Main Street and the half-block walk to the fishing pier, was furnished in all manner of rattan, with fixtures painted in a thick lacquered black and deep Chinese red. Even the kitchen stove, which we would inherit upon her passing in 1958, was a bright red.

The memories I retain of our regular visits to see our grandma at the Kenwood Hotel are mostly of the long trip getting there. It was one of the few places we traveled to beyond that tight L.A. hub of freeway interchanges. In the mid-1950s the Santa Ana freeway stopped short of completion and spilled out onto Beach Boulevard, which ran through miles upon miles of orange groves when Orange County truly was orange.

But the closest I came to knowing Grandma Hallie was in the last year of her life, when she lived with us for a short time under my mother's care after suffering a massive stroke. I remember my mother bathing the flaccid pale body of her mother-in-law in the tub. I remember the same sagging body on the toilet and my sister and I sitting sentinel at the old woman's feet. Waiting for our mother to wipe and fetch her, we three passed the time deciphering the stories hidden inside the design patterns on the linoleum floor. I liked that. I remember Hallie sitting at our small kitchen table for her morning coffee. I watched riveted, the cup rattling in its saucer as she raised it trembling and steered it into the open slit of her mouth.

With the death of Hallie Huff, our life as a family would take a dramatic turn. The Kenwood Hotel was passed on to Hallie's two children: our father and his sister, Barbara. For a brief stint Barbara, a divorcée with four children, managed the place. It seemed she failed at the post (I learned in whispers behind closed rattan doors) by sleeping with too many of the tenants. That's when our hero-mother, with a third-grade education and the wisdom of survival, would take the helm.

By the time we made the move in 1960, the hotel's heyday was long over, catering exclusively to wayward suicidal lovers, homosexual loners, thieving lesbians, and chain-smoking alcoholics. Well, that's how I understood it, as an eight-year-old, watching the dramas unfold all around me, my belly pressed against the smoke-saturated hallway carpet, as I expertly shot rubber bands at a lineup of green plastic WWII soldiers. My brother slaughtered me and I slaughtered Memo, a year younger, from apartment 14. I loved Memo, brushing my cheek up against the soft carpet of his crew cut whenever we played house.

During our time in Huntington Beach, my dad stayed on in South Pasadena to keep his job at the station. As both hotel manager and maid, Vera supported herself and her kids, fought off the advances of the single male tenants (of which there were many), and never asked her husband for a dime. Joseph would dutifully show up to spend one night a week with the family, sometimes punctuated by an evening out at the Paddock, a 1940s family cocktail-seafood restaurant, just across the street from the hotel.

I don't remember missing my dad. Sometimes in his absence, my sister and I would sleep with our mother, the "No/Vacancy" light flashing on and off and spilling its neon red or green over the bedspread. The sheer curtains would flutter with the summer's ocean breeze as the waning sounds of midnight partying faded in the distance.

On occasion, during those summer months, our dad would accompany us kids over to the beach. Stripping down to his swim trunks, he'd make a mad dash for the water, diving headlong into the formidable waves. He enjoyed swimming (something I never saw my mother do), but once out of the water, he was quick to dry himself off, and JoAnn and I would cover the full length of him with a beach towel, adding T-shirts and smaller towels for his extremities, burying his feet in the sand to shield them from the midday sun.

Most of the time, we three kids spent the whole day on the beach by ourselves, our skin easily darkening under the sun; we girls collecting soda bottles from teenaged beachgoers for the nickel and two-cent deposits they yielded. At the end of the day, dragging our booty-filled burlap sacks along the sand, we'd cash in their bottles for our own of Coca-Cola and Nesbitt's Orange soda pop.

On the best of beach days, a sandbar might unexpectedly emerge from the belly of the ocean, just past the breaking waves and dangerously near the barnacled legs of the Huntington Beach Pier. On such occasions, my big brother would lift me up on his eleven-year-old shoulders and carry me across to it, me holding all our towels up over my head to keep them dry, as our sister swam fearlessly alongside us.

"You can touch now," my brother would say, and I'd leap off his shoulders to feel the freshly swept wet sand beneath my feet. Spreading out our towels, the three of us would lie down on our bellies, sunning ourselves on a deserted island in the Pacific Ocean. It was our imagined paradise.

Paradise is lost on the morning our mom comes into our bedroom, sits on the edge of the bed, and announces that she is going into the hospital. "For a rest," she says. JoAnn is speechless. I cry. "No more than a week," she promises. But we both detect the lie.

That night, on the eve of her departure, fearing her doctor's suspicion that the growing pain in her stomach is cancer, Elvira goes to her altar and lights a votive candle before the portrait of San Antonio de Padua, clad in his Franciscan friar's garb, El Santo Niño in his arms. She promises to wear the robe and rope of her santo if he would only entreat God on her behalf. If only she might live just long enough to see her young children grown, just long enough for them to be raised by a mother who loves them like no one else will.

Querido San Antonio
Yo, con toda confianza, te invoco . . .

It was marvelous to behold, my mother told me of her first encounter with San Antonio. In 1940, upon her return from Tijuana, she had gone to see la curandera on the east side of town. She entered la sala, where an altar in San Antonio's honor filled the room. It was ablaze in candlelight, and the whole room was "so full of God" that Elvira literally dropped to her knees. "The lady could see things," she said. "She could tell your future." What she saw, my mother never said, but from that moment onward, Elvira never ceased in her devotion to the saint. To San Antonio we, as a Mexican family, prayed each day as we walked out the door, blessed by my mother's thumb and forefinger shaping a cross upon our foreheads. To San Antonio my mother offered up all that was inconsolable inside her.

During my mother's hospital stay, my mother's youngest sister, Eva, took us girls into her home with her family of six. Soon one week turned into another and another, until JoAnn and I were eventually enrolled in a nearby Montebello school. As I entered the third-grade classroom, the teacher handed me my very own personal box of school supplies. I liked the box, but feared it put my mother's return even further away. Back at my auntie's house, I secretly stole comfort in the sound of her voice from the kitchen, regañando a sus hijos. How I envied my cousins' scoldings, the familiar inflections in Spanish; the smells of home, ajo con comino; the cadence of a Mexican mother pounding out tortillas; the timbre of my tía's throaty laughter, so like my mom's.

Our brother had been sent to stay with Grama Dolores on Adams Street in L.A., a monolingual Spanish-speaking world, where our cousin David, a year younger than James, served as daily interpreter. We missed our brother. Something changed for James during that time (that's what his sisters think); when barely twelve years old, he could neither visit his could-be-dying mother nor did his father come to relieve him of his worry. He would return to his family more apart from us. More on his own.

Vera described her husband coming to visit her in the hospital. Was it daily? "But he might as well not've come at all," she'd tell me in the years ahead, before I was old enough to truly taste bitterness. "He'd just stand there in the room como un pendejo. He didn't have a damn thing to say to me!"

What *do* you want your husband to tell you when you are tied up in a knot of IVs and your three children have been distributed like chores among the relatives? What does a man say to his wife when she might very well die from whatever history is eating away at her gut? But my thirty-eight-year-old father had nothing to show or tell her of their children—no small anecdote, no hand-drawn get-well card—because he scarcely, if ever, saw them.

My father came of age in a kind of *Mad Men* world, minus the suits and the secretaries. He was a white man indistinguishable from the rest, whose only requirements were to bring home a paycheck and never lay a violent hand on his wife.

Only once did our father hit us. It is midafternoon when he enters the kitchen to the directive: "Go hit the kids." I don't know what we had done wrong—talked back, fought with each other, the usual stuff. Not once do I remember my mother saying, "Wait until your father gets home"; for she absolutely knew it was she we feared. But clearly this time Vera had had it! He comes into our bedroom, utterly awkward in his performance as disciplinarian. We stand in lineup, ready for the belt, but instead he begins to awkwardly slug at us with his fist, not knowing where or how to hit us. I remember being knocked on the head. His punches were heavy, but intentionally not hard enough to hurt. We all three held back our nervous laughter, so as not to embarrass him. It felt so strange because there was no anger in it. No anger meant no passion. And passion was what our mother had us kids understand as love.

"Mama's gonna die," JoAnn whispers. She couldn't keep the worry to herself. That morning she had overheard a phone call my auntie had received from the hospital. We had suspected it all along, never believed my mom when she said she was just going in for a rest. She had looked too, too sad. And scared.

Days before, our auntie had taken us out to buy new school clothes, dresses we could never afford at home. And, although every weekend their family went out to eat at nice restaurants, JoAnn and I felt that each new dress, each dinner out betrayed our mother, lying broke and broken in her hospital bed, a mere half-hour drive away.

At night, I would lie next to my sister on the pile of sleeping bags and blankets on the front room floor, praying for our mother's life. All night long, I scratched and scratched and scratched. My nails became pickaxes, digging away at the quarry of blood and pus and crusted flesh inside the fold of my arm. Missing her was unbearable.

In the daytime, death was postponed. My elbows snapped into switchblades as I wrapped a tomboy's grip onto a baseball bat, just like James had taught me. Where *was* my brother? My bat meets the ball as it flies over Tío Manuel's garage in the hope of my mother's return. Cousin Manuelito pulls off his baseball cap in amazement: *a girl who can really hit a ball!*

"She's not going to die. Your mother is having an operation." My auntie had rushed in, hearing my grief-stricken cries from the other room. Her eyes cut at my sister. But JoAnn knows that I am the bellwether. She throws me into the wind to catch the storm coming down the road.

"What kin'a operation?" I ask between hiccupped breaths.

"They have to take out a part of her stomach."

I fall onto the blankets, sobbing.

My auntie looks down at me and then suddenly exits. My sister cries quietly next to me. Moments later, Auntie Eva calls me into her bedroom. JoAnn clings to the doorjamb just outside the room, desperately hoping her little sister's tears will bring to her own numbing fear some assurance. Auntie Eva spreads out a thin white paper napkin over her palm. She picks up two diagonal corners and presses them together, then does so again with the opposite corners. It forms a small bag. "This is your mother's stomach," she tells me. I am transfixed by this little pocket of air. My mother's life depends on it. "What the doctor is going to do is take out just a small part of the stomach that is sick. Like this." She demonstrates, folding in one of the corners and reconnecting the rest into a puffy triangle. "And that's it."

I have never loved my auntie as much as I did at that moment, especially now, thinking about how afraid she herself was at the very real prospect of losing the one person on whom she could count. Elvira was more than a *second* mother to Eva.

The paper napkin demonstration had done the job. It quieted me down, although I would learn later that the "small part" turned out to be three-quarters of my mother's stomach and the "cancer" a peptic ulcer that would require a second surgery due to complications.

But Elvira survived it. More than a month later, my mother would stand in Eva's front room, her hands raised in the air, while la señora seamstress measured my mother's waistline and battle-scarred stomach. Her prayer answered, she would don the brown tela of San Antonio's Franciscan garb for a full month, a rope wrapped 'round her waist, in gratitude for saving her life.

"Obey your mother, so she doesn't end up in the hospital again." These were Auntie Eva's parting words as we piled into my dad's used Buick station wagon to make our way back to Huntington Beach. Barely recovered, my mother closes up our life at the Kenwood Hotel. And, in a matter of months, the place is put up for sale. Initially, my father was against it, having grown accustomed to the extra income my mother's management of the Kenwood had provided. But the ulcer in my mother's gut proved the enormous stress she had suffered to run the place (maybe it wasn't her daughters' fault after all) and my mother was adamant about the sale.

Throughout the eighteen months we lived in Huntington Beach, Vera had assumed that her husband had been putting money away for our return to South Pasadena. Without a family to support during our absence and having rented out one of the bedrooms to a single tenant, there had to be some savings. But no, Vera discovered, as she navigated her way through our once home, now unrecognizable due to neglect, Joseph "didn't have a damn penny to his name."

Aimless without his wife, he left bills unpaid, sink drains clogged, and year-old cereal boxes crawling with cockroaches. To make matters worse, the lingering threat of a lawsuit shadowed our return when he confessed to his wife that he was at fault for an auto accident involving an injury to an older female driver. He had let the insurance lapse, so upset was he by his wife's illness. This is how he explained it: the drinking, the recklessness, and the utter neglect; he had been "upset."

We are parked out in front of the injured party's house. Our parents are there to plead with the woman not to sue. My mother instructs us three kids to sit up tall in our seats, to look well behaved as they go to the door. When the Anglo lady opens the door, my father says a few brief words to her. The woman's eyes pass over my mother and then she quickly dismisses her, as my father is invited inside. Elvira is insulted, we can see it on her face coming down the walkway, but she does not say a word about the *pinche cabrona* until she gets back into the car. The wait seems endless. My mother fingers rosary beads. Finally, the lady and our father reappear at the front door. They step out onto the porch. We see our father indicate again the wife and the three children in the car, a last-ditch effort for her compassion. We sit up taller in our seats, affecting the somberness required. And then it is over. The lady returns into her house, and as my father comes back toward the car, we catch a small smile on his face and we know that as a family, we have prevailed. *But where did all the money go? Women, booze, gambling?* My mom both wanted and didn't want to know. And yet there was no real reason to believe that my father had been unfaithful to my mother in any way other than the neglect of his wife, his children, and our home.

The hotel sold quickly and the money was used as down payment for a house in nearby San Gabriel. But there was no celebration. Something had broken between my parents by the time we repacked our things and made what would be our family's final move to that mission town just three miles southeast.

THE OTHER SIDE OF THE TRACKS

For twenty-two years, México lived next door to us in the body of my forever-anciana grandmother, Dolores Rodríguez de Moraga. To live in proximity to my abuelita was to daily remember an América before Anglo intrusion. Born in 1888 in Sonora, México, but baptized in Florence, Arizona (the document of which she used as proof of U.S. citizenship), my abuelita remained faithful to her position as surviving matriarch of the family and to her mexicanismo until she passed in 1984.

The México my abuelita brought to my daily life was one of a Sonoran Desert of covered-wagon entrepreneurship and the high dusty drama of an untelevised West. She rides shotgun (without shotgun) at my grandfather's side, as they pull up into a Yaqui pueblo, pots and pans and kitchen utensils for sale clanking their arrival. The Yaqui families sit silently in a circle around the mestizo vendors. Nobody moves. The minutes pass slowly. Young Dolores grows impatient. "Vámonos, no quieren nada," she snaps at my twenty-year-old grandfather. He urges her to wait and watch. Many long minutes pass again until at last one man stands and approaches the wagon. Moments later, the whole community follows. Business was good that day for the newlywed Moragas.

The México my abuelita brought to my daily life was the length of her fingers threaded into the mouth of my antiwar folk guitar. She sang songs I do not remember the words to now, her voice a Chavela Vargas gravel, as she plucked at the strings with arthritic fingers having long lost the finesse of her girlhood musicianship. She came from una familia de músicos, she told me in her broken English. And yes, once, I remember seeing such a family portrait: the brass instruments resting across high-water woolen trousers, violins pressed against proud chests.

The México my abuelita brought was of familial memory, sleeping beneath the blond furniture headboard that held the small retrato of her long-dead mother, my bisabuela. At night with our evening prayers, we kissed the pursed mouth of the small sprig of a woman, clad in a black high-collared dress, a chonguito atop her head. Bisabuela had died in her nineties, as my abuelita would two decades later. Her mourning of her mother had never lessened as I watched her become the same pursed-mouthed figure as the one in the photo. The same figure my mother would assume in the last months of her life. Me, too, I imagine. Me, too, one day.

When Grama Dolores moved to San Gabriel in 1962, she had already spawned the makings of a full tribe of more than one hundred descendants: eight living children who birthed thirty-three grandchildren, who would birth sixty-five great-grandchildren and counting. Following her daughter Elvira, she left a South Central Los Angeles plagued by interracial conflicts—Black against Mexican against newly arrived Asian immigrant—that still afflict it today. My abuelita was reluctant to make the move until that fateful afternoon when poor eyesight reconfigured the light-skinned Black man who entered her bedroom to be her son Roberto. Holding a knife to her throat, he demanded she not make a move while he ran off through the rest of the house to scavenge for cash and anything of worth he could carry inside the deep pockets of his trousers. In the meantime, my abuelita, who was already in her seventies, crawled through the open window of her bedroom and dropped a full ten feet to the crabgrass beneath her, running to her youngest daughter's house for refuge.

Before her move to San Gabriel there had been one last L.A. apartment in a courtyard of one-bedrooms, surrounded by Chinese immigrants who sang scoldings to their children in Cantonese from their one-step stoops. But the Chinese court was a temporary stay until the Moraga clan, in one huge migratory wave, landed in el valle de San Gabriel. That first cluster of suburban towns just east of East Los Angeles—Montebello, Alhambra, Monterey Park, and San Gabriel itself, with its Mission and Catholic schools—became our own familial cosmos of first and second cousins, aunties and uncles, compadres y comadres.

With Abuelita as neighboring matriarch, our small home in San Gabriel would become the familial locus for the greater tribu Moraga for a full generation. Located just south of Las Tunas Drive (the dividing line between us and the affluent Anglo homes to the north), our Anglo-surnamed and Mexican-mothered household occupied a kind of holding zone between Gringolandia and the forgotten mestizo-indio herencia of the town. The Native origins of the region had long been absorbed, close to extinction, into the culture of landless "Mexicans" who now resided on the other side of the tracks of AngloAmerica, in the shadow of ever-expanding freeway interchanges.

◉

In 1961, the San Gabriel we had moved to already showed the markings of a ghost town. Our home, a stone's throw away from the Old Mission, sat upon what was no doubt a kind of extended Indian burial site where six thousand unmarked Tongva graves lay buried beneath the Mission grounds. Even our street address bore the name of that ardent and ruthless crusader of Native conversion, Junípero Serra, and provided a daily reminder of that epoch of Spanish Catholic invasion nearly two hundred years prior. I often wondered if it was not the historical consequence of the brutal colonization of Native California that had siphoned off from this town what little ánima it had left in the latter half of the twentieth century.

I remember, just days after my family's move to San Gabriel, we took a shortcut through the open field behind our house for our first day of Mission Grammar School. My mother is fully made-up and perfumed, flanked by her three children, pressed into freshly starched uniforms. My sister and I walk gingerly across the moist morning earth in an effort to retain the whiteness of our newly polished Catholic school oxfords. I can still picture that lush-earthed empty field and the after-school games it promised, the winter smog-red sun rising at its eastern gate. But within months, a huge apartment complex replaced the field, with endless barracks-like rows of carports lined up against the chain link of our backyard.

The dream of Suburban America required its residents to believe that posted city limits, railroad tracks, and tree-lined boulevards protected them from the color of violence in the inner city. In the case of San Gabriel, "color" had always been there in the Uto-Aztecan descendants of the region, now carrying Spanish surnames on the south side of the tracks. By the 1960s, those same Natives and their mestizo relations from the south had evolved from the filero-toting pachucos of the forties to become khaki-clad cholos, cruising over "las lomas de East Los" into el valle de San Gabriel. Soon after they started coming home in Army body bags and a president and a would-be president and a Baptist freedom preacher and a freedom fighter and another freedom fighter got shot dead, and the suburbs, we came to learn, would not protect us.

In the heyday of my childhood, Las Tunas Drive, the main street of the town, featured the Edwards Theater, where, for a 25-cent admission ticket, I could cast my pre-adolescent eyes upon Latina-esque Suzanne Pleshette's beckoning cleavage magnified on the big screen. Just down the block from there was Las Tunas Market, a three-block, three-times-a-day walk from our house, which my sister and younger cousin Cynthia and I obligingly trekked on errands for my mother or abuelita. The market was eventually replaced by Julie's bakery, which had come to replace the "Helms Man" who each afternoon had brought to our street chocolate-dipped doughnuts and éclairs drawn from six-foot-long drawers opening from the back of the Helms van.

A few blocks away stood a local library, the size and prefabricated look of a jump-strip market, which provided my sister and me with endless distraction during the long smog-laden summer months. Never the reader my sister was, I'd still manage to keep up with her bookworm record by reading athlete biographies a third the length of her *Wuthering Heights*. A block down from there stood a pharmacist-owned corner drugstore where I worked into my late teens for $1.50 an hour when the minimum wage was $1.65. This is also where I would snag my first and only can of spermicide foam just in case the condom didn't work.

Crossing city limits, Las Tunas Drive became Main Street, Alhambra. With a Woolworth's five-and-dime and a Lerner's dress shop, the 25-cent bus drive to Alhambra soon replaced our regular shopping trips to Downtown Los Angeles. But Alhambra could never replace the wonder of L.A.'s "Angel's Flight." As little girls, JoAnn and I had held tight to our mother's straight-lined skirt riding up a near ninety-degree angle on the famous funicular railway on Bunker Hill.

In short, life in San Gabriel along Las Tunas Drive and its vicinity was in many ways what it was intended to be: ordinary, a kind of Anyplace USA, without a memory bank to invest in. What was not ordinary to me was that San Gabriel was to provide the final stomping ground for that band of Mexicans—once españoles, once indios—that our familia would never be again.

By the turn into the twenty-first century, my parents' regular excursion to Dandy's, a coffee shop run by a Chinese woman, who called my parents "mama and papa," proved to be the highlight of the Las Tunas Drive experience. Catering to an aging Anglo and MexicanAmerican clientele and some younger Chicano familias, the budget meals provided a kind of landing spot for my parents where routine far outweighed the need for quality taste.

At the same time, in those final decades, San Gabriel had gradually become home to a near majority of Asian immigrants. Once, in the mid-nineties, passing the site of the old Del Mar Drive-In Theater, where we used to go as teenagers, now a huge Asian shopping mall, my mother declared, "And we [meaning Mexicans] have been here from the beginning and we don't got a damn thing to show for it." Did she feel the same way about Anglo incursion? I wondered, but imagined not, since Anglos had reigned as landlord in Alta California since the generation before her parents' birth. To my mother, Anglo incursion was law and preceded my mother's quiet protest by more than a century.

Anglo incursion was also the intimate matter of family, my mother being the first and only one of her generation to invite one

into her marriage bed, setting a trend for the generations that followed. But you can't really escape Mexicanism in California. In
my parents' final decades in San Gabriel, single-family houses were
largely replaced by particleboard apartment complexes, squeez-
ing eight families into a lot size that used to house one. Mexicans
began to return en masse to my childhood neighborhood and my
mother's position there returned to its origins. Young married
neighbors referred to her as "La Señora Vira," as she assumed the
role of la viejita de la vecindad, cuidando sus plantitas and serving
as resident consejera for abandoned wives and wayward children.
Culturally speaking, she ended up en el mismo mundo mexicano
en donde había empezado su vida.

JUST EAT YOUR CHICKEN

La fuerza de Elvira. I cast the character of my mother in Spanish because all that I understand as strong, as capable, as having principled values, resided first in the one-hundred-pound mestiza body of my mother. She was someone who could handle so much and so many in the world. In our extended familia, she served as the planet around which our near-hundred relations hovered like orbiting moons. Over the years, I came to realize that what had kept us all gravitating to the sphere of my mother's kitchen (aside from her incomparable chile colorado) was our shared sense de su fuerza incansable. She was not always right, but she was always, until the last years of her life, "present." In the very way my father was not.

As a little girl, I often watched my father's face above his daily cup of black coffee, his eyelids fluttering to a close in his inherent shyness in front of others. I would contemplate the lengthening space of his forehead with his receding hairline, searching for signs of soul, ánima. To us, our father was a kind of functionary, the breadwinner, the black steel lunch box that waited for him on the kitchen counter each afternoon. He was the hill of blankets and the stagnated smell of stale breath sleeping throughout the morning hours. *Keep your voice down, your father's sleeping.*

Culturally, he was guided in the ways of Mexicanism through his wife's insistence. In his later years, he would dutifully drive Grama's caretakers to and from their homes every weekend, filling the quiet of what was an interminable drive, for both him and "Maria," in a broken and awkward Spanglish. There was no hint of superiority in his dealings. My father entered his wife's culture without prejudice and with little need for defense of his own. He was our biological father, yes, but he did not fertilize the seeds of culture. This was my mother's task, to sow and hoe and grow us up with a Mexican heart in an AngloAmerica that had already occupied the village.

Elvira raised her children, and guided all those that came through her door for counsel, with a foundational set of values that can best be summed up in the phrase "No te dejes." *Don't get used . . . taken advantage of . . . abused.* Although not always told to me in Spanish, it was later that I learned that so much of what my mother taught her familia were translations from a worldview conjured from an invaded and fractured México, but one that proffered the welded tools for our survival in Gringolandia.

"No te dejes" didn't keep me from "experimenting," as my generation imagined itself doing during the liberation movements of the 1970s, but it did tell me when to leave the bar or the bed of a batterer. It reminded me to step away from the cruelty of gossip and to learn when to hold my own cruel tongue. It developed in me a fierce judge of character, one as tough on myself as on others. And finally, it made it very difficult to lie. It was not a "happy" childhood, but a true one, if for no other reason than I somehow believed myself loved, not only by my mother, but also by my entire familia mexicana.

◉

My tía Tencha and Elvira are nursing an hour's worth of Friday-night-paycheck beers at the nearby Skip Inn. Our heads stacked pyramid style at the back-alley screen door, JoAnn, cousin Cindy, and I peer into the smoky dusk of the late-afternoon bar, trying to distinguish the silhouettes of our mothers. I check for the feet first. As our eyes adjust to the dark, my auntie's iridescent feet, covered in her coveted aqua-colored pantuflas, gradually come into view, propped up on the leg of a barstool. She suffers from merciless bunions and, after eight hours of assembly-line work, the fluffy pastel slippers become their own kind of podiatric sanctuary.

The two are hardworking women who wave us off with "We're just gonna finish this one last beer, mi' jitas." And true to their word, even when the beer extends itself into another, they finally emerge in good humor, smelling of hops and Salem cigarettes and electronic copper wire. We make our way home to my auntie's house, stopping off at Nino's to order a small-size pizza for a buck fifty and a few RC Colas to split. Friday nights were the best of times, for they were off-the-clock times.

On most other days, JoAnn and I walk the two blocks home from Mission Grammar School, drop our books onto the Formica fake-wood dining room table, have a snack of maybe a buttered tortilla and a glass of frozen orange juice, and get to work.

First, we make everyone's bed, pick up the soiled clothes off the floor and stuff them into the hamper: men's and boys' pajama bottoms, boxer shorts, T-shirts. Then we wash and dry the breakfast dishes, wipe down the countertops, and sweep the kitchen floor. Then we collect and empty the trash around the house and shake out the throw rugs. We clean up the bathroom, hang up the towels, and put the cap on the toothpaste and the lid on the Listerine. We toss cleanser into the bowl of the sink. We scrub. Then we start our homework.

An hour or so later, our mom comes home tired and irritated from the electronics plant. The work quotas keep getting higher; the arthritic pain in her knuckles is killing her; they got a new forelady that is jealous that my mom is so well liked by the other workers. My mom brings them tortas, burritos de carne y cebolla, little special things she makes the night before.

Coming down the driveway, she had heard Grama cussing up a storm next door when one of the aunties starts some kind of pedo. The pleito always ends with my mom to blame somehow because she's the one who doesn't fight back. She just swallows it, my tías Vicky and Josie always stirring up trouble. "That's why she can never keep a husband," says my mom about Josie, the biggest troublemaker of them all. "She doesn't know how to keep her damn mouth shut."

My mom knows she should probably go over to Grama's apartment to settle the problem, but she's so sick 'n' tired of it all. She never gets a moment's rest, and does anybody give a damn? By Saturday, one or both of the two tías (if they are talking to each other) will turn up in our driveway with a six-pack of beer for an afternoon visit. We'll hear a voice calling from outside, "Elvira," all pleasant, like nothing has happened. That's when my mom will mutter to me something about how your mind just can't sweep away memories cuz it's the heart that remembers. I figure she's talking about the bad stuff. And I finish sweeping the last of the breakfast crumbs from the kitchen floor and head out the door for the toolbox. I am forever cleaning up and clearing out, hammering and fixing, raking and sweeping; my sister and I taping moldy tiles back up onto the crumbling bathtub wall and kitchen sink, covering up the broken spots.

After the tías have gone, my mom will make a perfect dinner. Tonight, it will be curry chicken Mexican-style, mashed potatoes, canned peas. The canned peas are not perfect, but my sister likes them. I just roll them around my plate to look like they've been eaten. Mr. Perry, the old man boarder who lives in the room behind the garage, sits at the chopping board that comes out like a drawer from the kitchen counter. It is covered by an embroidered flour sack to make a small tablecloth and I have folded the paper napkin into a triangle and put it on the right side of his plate with the knife and spoon on top. The fork will go on the other side. My mom taught us this from her Tijuana days. There Mr. Perry will eat his meal and drink his nightly buttermilk in silence. The buttermilk looks thick and delicious in its clear glass, but it's not. I think you only drink buttermilk if you grow up on a farm in Kansas like Mr. Perry. Mr. Perry's skin is paper-thin white and spotted purple and pink. His old man hands tremble when he brings the buttermilk to his lips and he has only one eye. He lost the other eye from skin cancer and from waiting too long to go to the doctors because Christian Scientists don't believe in them. But eventually he gave in and the missing eye is now just a hole in his head. Sometimes the patch covering the hole opens, which of course he can't see. But we can see it, a huge empty bowl carved out from the gray bone in the side of his face. We don't say anything, just eat our chicken.

My sister talks and talks while my brother and I eat fast. That's why JoAnn's so skinny, because she'd rather talk than eat, which gets my mom mad because she has to worry about her, giving her special tonics like cod liver oil so she'll fatten up. Our father doesn't eat with us because he always works overtime at the Hobart Railyard, usually the graveyard shift. That's the best pay for the hours.

After dinner, my sister and I will fight about whose turn it is to wash or dry the dishes, but we won't hold it against each other later. I think my brother does his homework while we fight. Or maybe he watches TV or goes out to play some ball. But he doesn't have to worry about school too much cuz he can do everything pretty much hands down, no sweat.

Later that night, my mom will be ironing in front of the TV. She unrolls the burritos of wet starched cotton and sprinkles them from a green-tinted Coke bottle with holes in the metal cap. JoAnn and I will be finishing our homework. Then we'll get to watch TV, too, like Million Dollar Movie *or* The Loretta Young Show, *and maybe my brother will join us and my mom will ask me to adjust the clothes-hanger antenna cuz I got just the right touch to make the snow almost completely disappear from the screen. And all three of them will cheer me on: "That's it, you got it. Hold it just like that!" And then I have to figure out how to let go without moving the hanger not even a fraction of an inch. Sometimes I just watch the TV from that spot, holding the antenna with my fingertips and twisting my head sideways around the TV to see the screen.*

We go to bed, maybe 10 p.m. or so, and we will say our prayers on our knees, sometimes with my mom, and then my sister will read and my brother will sleep (I guess that's what he does behind the vinyl-and-plastic accordion doors that separate his small twin bedroom from ours) and I will eventually fall out, too, to the sound of my sister reading aloud with true expression even when she whispers. I always promise I won't fall asleep, but her voice comes into my ear like a lullaby and it just drifts right into my dreams.

Maybe a half hour later or so, the whole house is asleep in the dark and I wake up, afraid that I have forgotten my prayers (although I haven't), and I will start my Our Fathers and Hail Marys all over again, just in case. And then I will nod off to sleep again and then I will wake up again, maybe an hour or so later, worrying that I forgot to check that all the windows and doors are locked. And I will get up oh so quietly so no one wakes up and tells me, "You're just crazy!" and "You're gonna make yourself sick!" Cuz they know and I know that I already checked everything too many times to be normal.

Like how it's not normal when my mom catches me at the kitchen table, waving my hand down below my right knee like I'm shooing a fly. At least that's what I tell her when she asks me, "What the hell are you doing?" So I gotta tell a lie cuz I can't admit that I might've just kissed the devil by accident. You know how when you're talking and you pause or something, how you naturally press your lips together and then they open again kinda like in a soft kiss. Well, I worry that God might think I want to kiss the devil, so I wave the air of that fall line to hell, where my kiss could've gone by mistake.

These are the things that keep me up at night. Until, finally, I fall asleep and dream the pictures I have been dreading all along—stupid "impure thoughts," like penises spraying menstrual blood and women's breasts all swollen like in those dirty magazine pictures. If the dreams wake me, and they always do, I'll sit up to pray some more and then get outta bed and check the doors again.

There were other nights I awoke to my father coming home after the bars had closed; nights I awoke to the sight of him crawling on all fours down the hallway, whining like a sick cat I once saw who had a fever that arched its back and weakened its limbs and caused a great animal cry to spill out from it. My father, too, looked fevered, and red-faced from so much alcohol, as he'd make a path down the hallway on his hands and knees to my bed. He'd try to kiss my cheek, but he smelled so bad and his nighttime beard was so scratchy, I'd pull away. So he'd just drop his heavy drunken head onto my blanketed belly, crying and begging for my pity because my mother was going to throw him out.

"I'm soooo sorry," he'd whine.

"Leave the girls alone," I'd hear my mother snap from her bedroom. And eventually he would. He never laid a hand on me. Just that head, that heavy head.

BODY MEMORY

MADRE: Have you met my son, God?

HIJA: Yes, I had a brother by the same name.

MADRE: Tell me.

HIJA: . . . What?

MADRE: Tell me about him.

HIJA: He's . . . I worshipped him.

MADRE: Yes?

HIJA: When we were young he'd play a game with me.

MADRE: ¿Cómo?

HIJA: He'd twist my arm behind my back and press it to the point of breaking.

MADRE: Oh.

HIJA: "Kneel down and call me God," he'd say. And so I'd whisper, "God." And he'd keep pressing until I'd say it louder and louder. And then—

MADRE: Dígame.

HIJA: He'd have me down to my knees, before I'd submit.

MADRE: You gave in.

HIJA: I had to . . . And then he'd let me go.
MADRE: I don't remember that.
HIJA: I know.

From *The Mathematics of Love*

There was the photo. It is a candid shot.

I am probably about four years old and I am sitting on my brother's lap. We are watching TV, my sister at one end of the couch; James and I are coupled at the other. The length of each of my bare legs straddles his bathrobe-clad thighs. The indoor shadowy quality of the black-and-white mid-fifties photo gives the impression of nighttime, just before bed. The photographer has caught us off guard, and this, no doubt, is what attracted his eye: the image of three children, immersed openmouthed in the ever-wonder of television circa 1956. Maybe it was an episode of *Lassie* or *Gunsmoke* or *Spin and Marty*; the moonlight of our faces reflects back the glow of the screen.

I had uncovered the picture, rummaging through an old box of long-abandoned family photos that my mother had kept on the bottom shelf of a kitchen cupboard. At first I see it as any adult might, as the original photographer had, as an image of childhood unselfconscious contentment. But upon closer observation, what draws my eye is the space of sofa between my sister at one end and the double-decker figure of my brother and me on the other.

The space told a story, which I had long ago suppressed, of a big brother's love and a little sister's reciprocity. Sitting down to watch TV, I had probably taken the middle spot between JoAnn and James; but, in the course of the evening, I had found my way onto my brother's lap. There was no objection on his part; he may even have drawn me to him. His head leans around mine for a clear view of the TV show. We are so close we adapt seamlessly to the other's body.

◉

I remember feeling myself the body of my brother as I tucked the football under my left arm and against my barely budding chest. I had his moves. He had trained me how to weave effortlessly to escape the tackler's grasp as my hips shifted from side to side and out of reach.

I remember feeling myself the body of my brother as I followed through with the basketball, wrist slapping down in the last flick of the shot, the ball swooshing through the hoop . . . again, effortlessly.

I remember the boxing gloves bound tight around my wrists, my brother's palms rubbing the backs of my shoulders—"You can do it, champ!"—as he pushes me into the ring for the fight.

I remember feeling myself the body of my brother the first time I grabbed a woman by the waist and escorted her out to the dance floor.

MARTIN

It is the day before my Confirmation, the Holy Sacrament through which I am to become a "Soldier of Christ" in a ceremony where the bishop will slap my face as a lesson in turning the other cheek. Sister Genevieve has just stepped out from our seventh-grade classroom and has disappeared down the hall. Our class of sixty-one hormonal females immediately falls into full and predictable chaos. Ten minutes later, seventy-year-old Genevieve will return, the crumbs of a morning pastry on her scapular, and will ask who had talked in her absence.

"Confess," she says. And, in order not to add the sin of lying by omission to the transgression of talking in class, I will stand up. Alone. And Sister Genevieve will make an example of me. I remain standing at my desk as she crosses to the blackboard to review the class Communion chart. She is aghast to discover the utter absence of silver stars next to my name: daily masses, yes, but not a single Communion. "What kind of sinner must you be?" she asks aloud.

When I enter, the midafternoon New Mission Church is mostly empty. A middle-aged man in grease-stained work clothes kneels in back, his face buried into brown swollen hands. A few devoted viejitas are praying; the thinning treads of their fingertips skim their rosaries like worry beads. I tip along the scuffed linoleum floor as the old women look up, scanning me with suspicion—or is it concern? Their lips murmur marías.

I cross to another aisle, genuflect, and scoot into the pew. I start to kneel, then stop. I sit back, my hands on the thighs of my blue-and-gray-checkered uniform skirt. I hesitate. It is my final face-to-face conversation with God.

I do not pray. Praying has not helped. I wait a long time to find the right words until all I can think to say is . . . "I give up."

This is the catch-22 game of Roman Catholicism. In order to receive the sacraments, you must be in the "state of grace." But you cannot be in the state of grace because, from minute to minute, second to second, you fall from grace. By thinking. By doubting. By having a body with too much boy in it—too much hair on your upper lip, your toes, your thighs, your belly, which you shave & pluck & bleach & wax away behind locked bathroom doors. Sinfully, you stuff the depilatory paraphernalia (hardened lumps of wax stuck against the walls of a bent metal saucepan) beneath towels in the far corner of a closet drawer. And your mind . . . your mind wanting females like a bandit.

You are not brave like Frank, the boy-girl in seventh grade strutting around open-legged in her uniform jumper (the sackcloth of a bitterly imposed penance). No, you are too smart, too sorta cute, too well raised to be a Frank. Frank, who is not Mexican, would not be loved, her rebellion told you. While you, the impostor, feign the good daughter, la niña obediente. But you can't fake it to God, and God made the Church's rules. And the Church will banish you, decree you outside the Mystical Body of Christ. So you will have to come clean with the impure thoughts that rack your sleep at night. But not to the priests, for the priests have already forsaken you.

In the dark shame of the confessional booth, the devil sits gluttonously pleased behind your left shoulder, where once your guardian angel stood. "Don't come back here," the priest says. (It is your fourth confession that week.) "You're crazy. You need to get some help." The confessional grille slams shut before your latticed shadowed face. You rise, push your weight against the huge oak doors, and step back out into your masquerade life.

By tomorrow you will have to say to everyone in the world that matters, "For two years now. It's been going on for more than two whole years." But you know you will never find the courage for such a public suicide. Instead you barter for the privacy of the communal church, where you beg God's counsel, a directive, or even an ordinary unannounced miracle to relieve you of your suffering—its desperate weariness, its aloneness. You sit in your Catholic school uniform. Your eyes lift up to the blond Christ hanging heavy-headed and impassive over the altar steps. And wait.

And wait.

And wait.

And then . . . nothing.

Just . . .

nothing.

There is no god out there.

And in the silence of that extended moment, the sensation of a pro-
found emptiness begins to move from the bottom of your belly. You
feel it rising gradually—a wave of something stirring, a fluttering just
beneath your rib cage, climbing until it spills open-winged and light as
breath into your chest. It is a presence, an almost-you, but not quite,
something grander and oh so ordinary at once. You, in the company
of the praying viejitas and the obrero in his grease-covered pants; you,
in the familial ecosystem of Elvira punching the time clock at the Elec-
trocube a few blocks away, of Tío Bobby picking up starched shirts
for his evening bartender shift, of Abuelita hanging sun-bleached
manteles out on the clothesline to dry. All of you warmed by the after-
noon sunlight spilling in through the stained glass just above your
head. So ordinary. Just heat and light and a kaleidoscope of color from
the window; and a vast and holding endlessness in your heart.

And you are suddenly, inexplicably, unafraid.

"I'm not fearing any man."

And you make a promise to yourself that you will meet every pan-
*icked impure thought with three words—*I am good. *Even if you*
don't believe it, even if you have to fake it all the way up those altar
steps to the bishop's slap and you will go on faking it for years to come
until you will finally, perhaps, come to know its truth.

I was not yet thirteen when I, at last, clawed my way out of the
hole of that perverse exile, nails dug into the earth of my own
crumbling self-abnegation. All the while, clinging to the rope of a
deeper knowing: that I was not truly condemned to the tyranny of
that hell my brain and church and traitor body had concocted.

And just as my head clears to catch a glimpse of a huge and
open sky and Martin's "promised land" beneath it, I spy my sister.
She, the Jill who comes tumbling after me. And I catch her, you
see, *before* she drops into that abyss. I say, out of love for us both,

"Don't believe it, JoAnn. Don't believe those ugly thoughts. They're just thoughts," I say, full of doubt. "You're good, my sister."

And I know nothing about psychology, nor the "pedagogy of the oppressed." I know nothing about the origins of guilt 'cept Adam and Eve, and my feminism is a good ten years down the road, and my Buddhism another twenty, and unlocking the sad shame of Elvira will take another forty; but I do know that my sister and I were just plain guilty for being female, perhaps simply being females with hope; for feeling that we had a right to hope.

⊙

Two years later, I hear the Preacher's speech:

"I've been to the mountaintop." His voice trembled with the knowledge.

And I think—*Yes, that's how it feels.*

Martin Luther King, Jr., was a man of doubt who believed in freedom. And the faith of a man of doubt is stronger because it has been tested. Is tested over and over again.

"Like anybody, I would like to live a long life." The Preacher-Prophet knows what's coming.

And that's all courage really is. To move forward in the face of doubt, in the face of death. I would be free.

High school would be like that: my quiet refusal to suffer use-lessly while daily I witnessed my mother trapped in a memory maze of her own troubles. She having lost huge chunks of her life filling in the holes of an absent father, a dead brother, a widowed mother's forgotten mothering. Elvira, with a husband so dis-tant, so detached. Her constant nagging, the useless lid on a cauldron of brewing resentment.

Maybe I was just done with the tears, with my mother's inability to change, to give up the stories that caused her so much grief. Her refusal to stand up for herself and require a different life of her husband, of her never-satisfied mother, and, one day, of her son. I walked out of that kitchen with the righteousness of the young, when we still believe change is possible in the ones we love.

"You're just like the rest of them." Elvira throws the blade at my back. "You don't know how to love."

I keep walking.

MISSION GIRLS

My sister was not a lesbian, but she loved the nuns and our female teachers much more than I did. Still, I frame my high school years as a study in desire, around and about the nuns, my attraction to and contempt for them. There was the exceptional Sister Miriam Rose with the courage to leave the Dominican order. She was only one who ever said to me, "You can write. You are a good writer," even as my reading faltered.

JoAnn was the reader, a madrigal singer, and a diligent student. She needed school more than I did. She needed the company of those women. Our home was a place where homework wasn't especially honored, where good grades meant less than good housekeeping. While I excelled only in the latter, my sister, on Saturday mornings, lingered by our small bedroom bookshelf. Passing the dustrag over the painted plywood with one hand, she would turn the pages of a library book with the other.

A memory shelved somewhere returns me to a time.

I am a junior in high school. I sit tall on the office counter stool, fingering the attendance-record cards in a long file box. I make my marks. It is my after-school job to pay for my tuition. I so much prefer it to my freshman and sophomore Saturday-morning jobs, following the quite elderly Sister Anita around, cleaning the home economics room and dusting library bookshelves. I knew it was a problem—how well I could clean. "I've never had a girl as good as you," Sister Anita would regularly remind me. I feared that my mother's home training had me doomed to the dungeons of such uninspired and isolating labor. But, by junior year, Winona, the odd girl with whom I had a yearlong no-touch lesbian relationship, graduated and had passed on to me the much more prestigious position of maintaining the school's attendance records.

Winona was a poet and an artist and she would secretly send me carefully scripted melancholic love poems in equally careful pen-and-ink calligraphy. I remember once when, after much begging, my mother allowed me to spend the night at Winona's house. (A very un-Mexican thing to do, since, as my mother always reminded us, *Tienes una cama en tu propia casa, so why do you got to go sleep in somebody else's house?*)

That evening, Winona and I lie down in our respective twin beds. It has been a good day of sharing clandestine writings and Winona's preoccupations with this or that nun. Once in bed, however, there is a long uneasy silence. I stare at the colorless ceiling when Winona says to me, "I wish I could just touch you."

And I feel a sudden and inexplicable revulsion. Was it homophobia?

I was attracted to Winona's lesbianism, but not to her. I often wondered what would have happened had her best friend, Tina, been the one to say those same words to me. Would I have climbed over that carpeted divide and into *her* twin bed?

Months before, on the last day of the school year, Tina and I had said goodbye for the summer. We held a hug, her white uniformed breast pressed against mine, and I walked the two blocks home replaying in my mind its soft weight, its fullness against my chest.

I enter the house, grateful that it is empty. I do not want to forget the feeling, even as I carry it heavily down the hallway. I drag myself into my unmade bed, twist the sheet tight into a rope and pull it up between my legs. And I just cry and cry and cry because my desire is so fucking, and undeniably, physical.

Tragedy befell Winona (or at least that was how I thought of it) when after graduation she entered the nunnery. It is the late 1960s and just as nuns all over the country are leaving the convent in droves, Winona decides to enlist. It was to be a lesbian, I knew, and I hated the thought of it. Repression as religion. These were my fierce convictions as a teenager, full of contradiction and tainted by fear.

When I visited Winona at the convent (and I did so only once), I knew this was the real masquerade; the whole thing, a performance. Sitting in a hard-backed chair, she held her hands quietly in her lap, her tidy little novice headpiece holding back her once-long hippie hair. She spoke in soft tones in a kindly manner. *What happened to my tortured artist beatnik friend?*

It is four twenty on the office clock. I am doing what I am supposed to be doing: working. JoAnn is doing what she is not supposed to be doing: not working. The attendance job is a breeze and I love the company. JoAnn should be home by now, cleaning house, awaiting our mother's return from the electronics plant. But she is caught up in the moment, in teenage-girl banter with the principal, Sister Mara, and a few other after-hours girls.

Mara is not so much a principal at the moment, but a woman—a grown and brown woman, who treats us with interest. For a moment, we are free and intelligent women with our futures beckoning just outside the threshold of that small Mission High School girls'-wing office. And we got nothing better to do. We got all the time in the world to just hang out and laugh and gossip about some silliness, some smart-aleck remark, some (dare I say even emergent-feminist) critique about the Church. We, women, so superior in vantage point, so presciently awaiting that second coming where God is indeed and justifiably a woman. Even when we have no words to say so.

And then without warning, the doorway darkens and our eyes land upon the sudden presence of . . . *Elvira*. JoAnn is closest to the doorway. She spots our mother first. I put my head down, am dutiful at my post with the attendance records. Mara stands sentinel to the scenario. Suddenly everyone else disappears.

I spy the leather belt held in our mother's crooked grip. JoAnn must see it, too. It hangs pulsing by her leg. *What is she thinking? Is she going to beat JoAnn like a wayward burra all the way back to the village?*

No, this was wrong—a private moment gone public. The equilibrium of our girlhood life had suddenly gone awry. Elvira and "the belt" were meant to remain on the *other* side of the kitchen doorjamb. *That* scenario we understood:

"Ven pa'ca," she would command us.

"No, Mom, you're gonna hit me."

"I won't hit you"—the lie of the belt, snakelike and writhing with intent along her thigh. And each time, no matter how many times she lied, we would cross that threshold to our own demise.

JoAnn does not bother to wait for our mother to lift the belt; she rushes by her and heads directly for home. She does not run off in a different direction, as perhaps other, less dutiful daughters might; for there is nowhere else to go but to that home.

◉

There had once been a grandmother, the American one, who thought JoAnn special, who allowed her always the foreground spot in the family photos, JoAnn's hair in thick ringlets falling upon her Easter outfit shoulders. Grandma Hallie had always defended her; for, like Hallie herself, who aspired all the way to the Geary Theater stage, JoAnn was a dreamer.

"But I don't got nothing to wear." JoAnn stares at our bedroom closet, where dresses from holidays past hang bored and styleless.

Dressing for Sunday Mass, Elvira can hear her eldest daughter through the bathroom vent complaining como si fuera una reina, like money grows on trees.

"Cállate, ya," she snaps back. "Put on anything, I don't got time for this."

Elvira wishes she could just shut the girl's face up, once and for all, that mouth of too-many-teeth always whining. She's like him, a husband who only knows to think of himself, who asks for a cup of coffee with his eyes like worthless hands.

"But I look stupid in everything." JoAnn says the wrong thing.

Esto es el colmo, the last straw. It is the moment our menopausal mother has been waiting for—a reason, any reason, really, to explode from that bathroom and let la ingrata have it.

"Ya te dije que no me friegues."

Elvira spills into the bedroom, wearing only a skirt, her breasts bare. She brandishes a hairbrush as a weapon. Against what?

Against Seventeen *magazine and Hollywood dreams?*

Against dreams?

Elvira never got to dream, cabrona.

She rushes at JoAnn, begins to beat her with the wooden back of the brush. I stand rigid, taking in the scene. JoAnn's arms flail in self-defense, falling onto the bed to block the blows. Elvira tosses the brush, spins around, and lunges backwards onto her daughter's head. Her small hips and bony nalgas pound JoAnn's face into the bed. Tailbone against jawbone, she pounds, over and over again.

"Stop, Mom," I cry. "You're gonna kill her."

But she doesn't stop, so I do what I have never done before. I stop her myself. I am as tall as my mother by then and strong enough.

I grab Elvira by the shoulders and pull her off JoAnn's crumpled face.

Elvira stands speechless before her teen daughters. Suddenly, realizing her nakedness, she picks up my bathrobe from the bed and drapes it over the front of her, one small breast exposed like a defeated Amazon. But I can't get the sight of those flaming purple nipples out of my mind; can't forget the hardened look of them—that bark of oak, the deep wooden grain of her anger.

"Get dressed," she says. "I'm going back into the bathroom and I'm gonna put on my face and when I come out, you both better be ready for church."

But I did not want my mother to put her face back on. My mother eyes me, as she moves to the door. I don't hate her. Somehow she knows this. My face has a grown gaze, but it does not wholly indict. She will come to count on this.

I don't remember what my sister's face looked like.

◉

As JoAnn pushes through the giant mission oak front doors, she flashes back on the sight of her younger sister jumping down from the office stool to block the path of their mother. It was the shield that allowed JoAnn exit. She didn't stick around to hear Elvira go into her litany of contempt. JoAnn's heart had already memorized the lines: *She might act like she's someone special at the school, but she's not so special, you don' know what she's really like . . .*

"Mom, please . . ." She hears her sister's receding voice entreating. The belt gradually slips back under Elvira's apron, as JoAnn's hurried feet beat the hot pavement home.

In JoAnn's defense, Sister Mara is all compassion with our mother. She has handled this before. She does not judge. She sends Elvira home, humbled but not shamed. Mara was a Mexican daughter, too.

MIND-FIELD

The college's good Catholic name had conveniently disguised to my family its subversive intent; perhaps until my graduation ceremony belied it, as barefoot girls with flowery crowns in their hair and a guy in a gorilla suit came onstage to accept their diplomas. (The gorilla got a banana.) Consisting of no more than some five hundred students, Immaculate Heart College stood white and deceptively mission-tiled on a hilltop overlooking a Hollywood Boulevard with its heyday in decay.

Those four years at IHC unwittingly laid stepping-stones to my eventual departure from Southern California. Although JoAnn also attended IHC, she and I had grown more distant. The half-hour commute from our home in San Gabriel to the radical IHC campus in the Hollywood Hills crossed a "mind-field" of class and cultural fronteras that stunned each of us into a kind of emotional paralysis.

A nagging uncertainty plagued me—about my womanhood, my sexuality, my mixed-blood ethnicity, all of which I had yet to fully acknowledge. It seemed I would not, could not be loved. Not only because I suspected I was a lesbian, but also because, against my family's wishes, I wanted to be free. But if free looked like my gringo classmates in their tattered and patched hippie costumes of downward mobility, if free required weekly acid trips and mota on most days, if free meant a complete and utter disregard for the labor of your elders while you dug your hand in their pockets for loose bills, if free was that cavalier male sense of entitlement and "cool" meant you had to sleep with it, then my freedom road was desperately uncharted and unpeopled. I instinctually avoided entering into any intimate relationships with other students. Only in the neutrality of the classroom did I find voice for questions that were generating viscerally from my body.

For the first time in my life, I read in earnest: the existentialism of Sartre and Camus (*The Stranger*); William Carlos Williams's *Paterson* and Walt Whitman's *Leaves of Grass*; Ray Bradbury's sci-fi and George Orwell's prophetic *1984*; the early feminist inquiries of Sexton, Plath, and Adrienne Rich; Beckett and Ionesco's Theatre of the Absurd; Carl Jung's "collective unconscious"; and Simone de Beauvoir's "second sex." All this as a way to chart out a worldview by which I might one day build a life. All white writers and mostly men.

Although small in enrollment, the newly nonsectarian and coed college opened my mind to a grand landscape far beyond the confines of my mission school education. The Immaculate Heart nuns were the first religious order in the country to cast off their religious habits and don secular clothing to better serve a spiritually motivated social activism. It was a terrible beauty, the education unfolding before me, even as it frightened me. For, unlike most Roman Catholic colleges of its days, Immaculate Heart was founded in the spirit of women's right to know and to act on that knowledge.

The spring semester of my sophomore year at IHC had been the hardest. My transcript from that period, as I remember it, was riddled with Cs and failing course withdrawals. One early April afternoon, returning from our daily commute, JoAnn and I pull up in front of our family home. It is a sunny day and the lavender petals of la jacaranda fall lightly onto the windshield. But I know no such lightness within me. I turn off the engine and JoAnn starts to get out. I grab her knee.

"Wait. I wanna tell you something." I feel her eyes on me.

"Okay," she says. And shuts the door.

I have both hands on the steering wheel, clenching it. I can't look at her. I begin, a feebly thrown lifeline.

"I think I am a homosexual."

I had never uttered those words aloud.

It was a short conversation, as I remember it. Her response was almost perfunctory; a weak wall against a swelling wave of trepidation inside her. *What will this mean about the rest of our lives?* Wisely, she suggested a therapist, Liz Broome, who had been her psychology teacher at IHC. But, personally, she admitted she needed to keep her distance. We were too close, she said, and reminded me of my preteen years when my wordless fear stirred sleeplessly in the bed next to her. The gallows rope of those pubescent predawn wanderings, locking and relocking doors, had threatened to hang her, too.

We both agreed.

And I am alone.

Dr. Elizabeth Broome greets me with a solid handshake. She is an attractive and formidable figure, middle-aged, light makeup and modern; but there is some sense of old-country peasant stock in her bearing, which comforts me. We take our seats. After a short and seemingly endless silence, I realize it's on me to speak first. I am afraid but I am more afraid of not speaking. I shove the words from my mouth for the second time in my life: "I think I might be homosexual." I don't know any other way to say it.

Another pause.

"And . . . ?" Her eyes do not leave my face.

What? I'm thinking, *That's the point. End of story. Life over.*

"If you are, what does that mean to you?"

"Well, I guess it means I gotta go get a woman."

I remember Liz Broome smiling at my response. I, too, heard how silly it sounded, like there was a lineup of lesbians along Hollywood Boulevard, just waiting for me to come along and pick one out. She crosses her stockinged legs and takes a long drag from her cigarette. I was in love with Liz Broome ten minutes into our first meeting.

She continued. "Do you have someone in mind?"

Normal. She's talking like this is normal.

"No. But I have a boyfriend."

And that, of course, had been the problem, that heterosex had reopened the corral holding back my longing for women and the stallions were now running wild inside me.

I understand drinking. I understand just wanting to make yourself so fucking numb that all that comes at you—the neon whirlwind of 1971 Underground Atlanta nightlife, the boyfriend with his army naked buzz cut holding you tight as you both weave your teenaged bodies from bar to bar, the daiquiris like snow cones freezing your young grip—is of no real consequence or meaning. I understand drinking, falling into the motel bed and onto the wide plateau of flesh beneath you. Sex. Sex that someone else is having, and no amount of fucking can beat out the sad.

Sitting in front of Elizabeth Broome in her professor's skirt, crossed legs and ever-generous gaze, I am disarmed. There was no real body to be, no real "me" to love, and Liz Broome went right to that place. "That's what we will work on," she said, concluding our first session. *My god, there is a "we" in this.*

In the short time I met with Broome she charged me exactly one dollar per session, "just to keep it professional." That's an eight-dollar psychotherapy bill for the last eight weeks of the semester (and a few freely offered phone sessions). I remember the phone sessions best. Each time, sneaking out to my father's small office behind the garage. Each time, my heart hammering up into my throat, as I dialed Broome's number, inserting my forefinger into the menacing face of the rotary phone.

"I'm falling, I'm slipping away." I had no other language to express my sense of entrapment; the recurrence of my preteen obsessions, the inability to fully inhabit the body I carried.

Each time, her response was the same.

"What do you see around you?" She would ask me to name the red geranium planted in a rusting Folgers coffee can; the climbing sweet pea flowers that Elvira had strung just outside the door's window; the framed picture of the Navajo horseman in a Canyon de Chelly landscape. My eyes would fall upon the small pad of white paper with my father's notes of scribbled numbers and his signature all-cap lettering, his nubby charcoal-brown cardigan hung over the back of a metal chair, and the browning water stain in the drop-ceiling tile just above my head.

"Every time you start to go," she'd say, "just stop. Come back by naming the things around you."

And it *would*, each time, bring me back to earth.

Eight weeks that saved my life. She never asked me if I had thought of suicide or if I wanted meds—standard questions directed at queer youth today. I used to wonder about this later when I recall how desperately lonely I was. But survival was bred into the Mexican character of my life. And somehow Broome knew this. She knew how "ill" I was when nothing in my history could express it. The despairingly lonely out-of-body sensation of Sylvia Plath's *Bell Jar*, a book that so many young women were devouring at the time, was a kind of approximation, but I was a *Mexican*American and the daughter of a woman who had unwittingly instructed me on the complex desire of women. I was not supposed to know and want what I knew.

Most of what I now remember of my time with Boyfriend, which would last for a full four years, was fog. A coastal fog that would not lift, that sank to sea level, that hung like a great gauzy cloud of hopelessness down to the kneecaps. Months into our relationship, as the Vietnam War was winding down but the lottery draft remained in operation, Boyfriend was drafted and, after a short stint in Augusta, Georgia, he was transferred to Fort Ord army base in the mist-soaked town of Seaside, California.

The benefit, for me, was that my active-duty heterosexuality was pretty much reduced to occasional clandestine weekends in nearby Monterey. But sex was not so much the issue as my heart. I had sequestered its feeling inside an inconstant body whose sexual longing erupted at the site of my own cleavaged breast and the look of young lust in Boyfriend's eyes.

I wanted to *be* him.

Driving past military stockpiles on Fort Ord's beachfront properties, I studied the handful of draftees keeping guard, rifles over their indifferent shoulders. They were the picture of my own lonesomeness. I was trapped like them, waiting out my time between the sheets with a kind and simple-hearted working-class boy who carried an inherited South Dakotan don't-rock-the-boat acceptance (not too unlike my father).

During that time, JoAnn and I had afforded ourselves a brief hiatus from living at home when we moved into a studio apartment on Franklin Avenue in Hollywood. Our excuse: a closer commute to college. Upon my return from those Monterey trips, I would sit on the floor, press my spine up against the closet bureau, cup my ears with my stereo headphones, and play Carole King's *Tapestry* album over and over again. "When you're down and troubled and you need some loving care," she sang. And in that private place, I made love to Carole King's voice. This was my freedom road. And although it looked like nothing but a dead end at the time, marriage was worse. And impossible.

To say this was one of the most miserable times of my life would have done little to assuage my mother's grief, had she fully known about my sex life. What she had worked so hard to preserve as a teenager, working the casinos of Tijuana, I squandered in rebellion and despair.

By the end of that fall semester, JoAnn graduated early, and we ended up returning home upon her engagement to a "nice Jewish boy" from the west side. She wanted to do it "the right way," she told me, to leave her mother's home and move directly into married life.

I didn't really want my sister to get married and had hoped, against all evidence to the contrary, that she might accompany me on my freedom road. Sadly, I never made that road look very enticing—or free.

For my sister and me, whose worldview bounded itself firmly in the working-class culture of the *east* side of Los Angeles, JoAnn's engagement to the young Jewish man with a college degree from the *west* side held its own promise of change. JoAnn had already drifted from the Church by then, having witnessed, during her years as an office clerk for the mission rectory, the hypocrisies of its male clergy—the drunkenness, the sexual and financial improprieties.

I only knew that the rules of the Church were rules I could no longer live by. We had both said as much to our worldly mother, for her faith had already shown us that "God" had very little to do with Church rules or rafters. So there was little surprise when, upon JoAnn's announcement that hers was to be a Jewish wedding, my mother responded, "You do what you want, mi'ja; there is only one God."

Once we moved back home, I began to plot my escape, not out of the Valley (not yet), but out of my parents' house and *before* JoAnn married. Afterwards, there would be no way out except to follow in JoAnn's marital footsteps or remain the perennial soltera viviendo con sus padres, living her sexual life on the sly.

I had a relative who did it: got herself a job in the factory and then got herself the girlfriend, whom she met at la fábrica, and moved her in con la mamá. It was a life: a perfectly acceptable MexicanAmerican life that has been going on at least since World War II and "Rosita la Riveter." Except for one detallito—it had a "don't ask, don't tell" policy. Nobody was out of the closet.

This is as if to suggest that at the age of twenty, I could realistically imagine a lesbian life at home or anywhere. I didn't *want* to be a lesbian. But equally, I didn't want to live in the prison of what today academics call "heteronormativity." Which brings me to the question of class privilege and Mexicanism. I don't remember meeting a bona fide educated middle-class MexicanAmerican (with the exception of the nuns) until long after I had graduated from college. Ours was the first generation to benefit from affirmative action (brief as it was), but it takes more than a generation to secure class ascendancy.

In the 1970s, my sense of class ascendancy was integrally tied to education. My siblings and I and a handful of first and second cousins were the first in our family to finish college. Education was freedom. My mother had instilled this drive for education in her three children, but by freedom, I imagine she meant economic access and the lifestyle privileges it affords. What she wasn't aware of was the type of freedom the gringo schools had taught us.

"Go wipe the streets with it" had been my mother's refrain to us in her most desperate moments, when the world we inhabited as emerging women in the social-change era of the early seventies meant to her the abnegation of every value of sexual self-preservation she had striven to teach us.

Once, after JoAnn's engagement, she had wanted to take a drive out to West Los Angeles to visit her fiancé. My mother wouldn't allow it.

"No," she said, and that was the final word.

There was no real logic behind my mother's decision. As I saw it, overhearing this transaction from my bedroom, my mother's no was arbitrary and unjust. JoAnn was already twenty-two, had finished college, worked full-time, and had finished any and all house chores that my mother had required of her for the day. But my vantage point was that of an "American" twenty-year-old of the early 1970s; not one where the betrothed daughters of nineteenth-century SpanishAmérica sat patiently among las aunties y la abuelita idly embroidering their days up to their wedding (a scenario my urban-based sole-income-provider mother was, herself, never able to fully enact).

Still, as the saying goes, and one to which my mother absolutely subscribed, "As long as you live in my house, you follow my rules." And, "If you don't like it, there's the door, señorita." Elvira was holding out for what she still hoped was my sister's virginity, or at least the pretext thereof, her wedding barely a few months away. The stakes were that high. "Pack your bags," she says. "Cuz if you leave the house right now, don't bother coming home." And with that, JoAnn returns to our bedroom, leaving the door slightly ajar. We were not allowed to close it. Not completely.

I think now, as a parent, about how my own kids by middle school insisted on a closed bedroom door, asserting their right to privacy; a word not only unmentioned in the Elvira-headed household, but virtually unimagined. To my mother, a closed door was a direct insult. Nothing good could happen behind a closed door, where daughters kept secrets from the mother.

It was an impasse. My sister all dressed up and nowhere to go, and my mother slamming pots and pans in the kitchen within earshot through the half-closed door.

I urge my sister, "She's bluffing. You gotta stand up to her."

So JoAnn, not fully convinced, begins to pack a small overnight case. The quiet draws my mother back into the room, ready for round two. Elvira catches her in the act.

"Wipe the streets with it, if that's what you want. Is that what you want?"

"No."

"Go 'head, sinvergüenza. I'll tell the boy's mother about the kind of girl you are. And you're not taking the car, me oyes?"

And then I insert, "That's okay, JoAnn. I'll drive you."

This is the breaking point. We are just too big to belt. Elvira's hands land like claws onto the bedspreads of the twin beds, tearing at the blankets and stripping the sheets beneath them. In a frenzy, she tosses pillows, pulls books from their shelves and knickknacks off the bureau, cussing up a tempest of fury. JoAnn and I stand by in disbelief.

Then we look over to each other.

I mouth to JoAnn, "Go."

She picks up the overnight case, slowly starts toward the front room, a dreaded mission to which she has been assigned. As she begins to open the door, my mother rushes down the hallway after her and pushes her way into its threshold, throwing her arms out to block JoAnn's exit.

It is a standoff, but Elvira is already weakening, in a flood of tears.

JoAnn carefully squeezes by her.

I follow.

And the two sisters get into the car.

The older one cries like it is the end of her life. The younger one starts up the engine, sensing it is a beginning.

DON'T ASK, DON'T TELL

ou're leaving with a secret."

My mother's words grab me by the throat. The phone falls to my chest. I am twenty-three years old. And this is what I know of a black hole. Her statement foretells my exile. She is losing me. She knows it. And into the dark firmament of that silence Elvira, the braver of us, has ventured.

I can lie and continue on without her or tell her the truth and . . . *and what?*

My Echo Park apartment had been thoroughly vacated, except for an overnight bag. It was my father's birthday and I called my mother to let her know that I would be arriving in the late afternoon for the family barbecue. For nearly three years, I had been spending less and less time with my family and more and more time in the lesbian life of Los Angeles: Silver Lake, Hollywood, Venice Beach, Echo Park . . .

"I . . . I can't tell you, Mom. You won't accept it."

I immediately detect the rising bitterness in her voice, which I understand as fear. "What could it be? I've been through everything with you already."

And she had. We both could run through the list of my transgressions since I started college: at eighteen, my refusal to keep going to church; my preference for pants over any kind of skirt; the announcement, with Boyfriend standing oh-so-brave and six-foot-small in the kitchen of my mother's resistance—"Cherríe and I are planning to move in together." She slams out of the room, unable to face the verdict of such scandal before the Moraga family jury. And then came the long cross-country trips with questionable female company.

"No, Mom," I say, the phone cord a shrinking connection between us. "This one is just too hard."

And that's all I have to say when a great wail erupts from her throat. "No, mi'jita!" she cries. "No me digas esto. Not that. No puede ser."

She is dying. This is how it sounds to me over the telephone line. Her grief rips open my chest when I suddenly realize, *No, it is me. I am the one who is dying.* My mother's llanto tells me so. This is what La Llorona sounds like. There is no mistaking it. It is the cry of a mother mourning the loss of her child. But how is it I can be standing with the phone in my hand and be dying at the same time? I stare at the parquet floor. This is what I feared as a child, bolting doors and nodding off to an endless stream of useless prayers; that who I was would mean the end to all I knew as familia.

I mourn the loss, not for myself, but for her.

"I'm sorry, Mamá," I cry back. "I'm so sorry to hurt you."

Suddenly there is a shift in her. It feels strategic. As my mother, she will try every tactic in her arsenal to protect her daughter from this path of heartbreak, to protect her daughter from abuse, from loneliness, from drug and alcohol addiction, from the sorrow she imagines such a life will bring me.

She accuses others of influencing me.

She accuses me of running around with the wrong kind of people.

She calls me weak, when she knows me strong.

A follower, when she knows I am a leader.

Until finally, she draws out the last weapon of her defense. "How can you get *satisfaction* from a woman?"

She throws the word at me—*satisfaction*—a switchblade nastier than any pelvis-thrusting Mick Jagger could conjure. And it is the best thing she could've said. Because I had suffered too long and too hard for the right to love, and not even my mother was going to make me feel dirty for it.

I would not abandon myself.

"That's none of your business," I say.

She is silent. And into the aperture of that silence, I insert the truest thing I can think to add.

"Don't make me choose, Mamá. Because if I have to choose between this life and my family, I have to choose my life."

And then . . . that's it. There is no more fight. I hear it through the quiet of the phone receiver.

I wait.

Until she speaks, all the fury in her voice gone . . .

"How could you think that there is anything in this life you could do that you wouldn't be my daughter?"

And that's it.

My mother would continue to suffer my often poor choice in girlfriends; my unreliable interstate car trips and backpack adventures; my solo sojourns to México; my sometimes precarious inner-city dwellings in New York, Boston, Oakland, San Francisco; my too many months away from her without a visit or too many weeks without a phone call; my political activism where in every evening news protest, she anxiously looked for my hollering face among the crowd. But we did not lose each other by pretending we were other than who we were.

That night after the birthday barbecue and the familia had all gone home, my parents would walk along our gravelly driveway and watch me back my car out, following it and waving goodbye, until I was out of sight. As always, the last thing I saw as I spun my car into the street was my mother blessing the air of my passage with a prayer for my protection.

The next day, I would travel El Camino Real (The Royal Road) from Los Angeles to San Francisco, ironically retracing the steps of the very missionaries I was fleeing. It was 1977 and for this MexicanAmerican once Catholic daughter, Highway 101 was not royal but "real." I had left that mission town of San Gabriel, having told my truth.

The truth *will* set you free. But, as the young philosopher* wrote, "not until it is finished with you."

My mother had made sure of that.

* David Foster Wallace.

PART II

NOTHING MÉXICO COULDN'T CURE

Mi'ja, do you know where this is?" Elvira pulls from her purse a folded airplane napkin smudged with ballpoint writing, and hands it to me. A lady sitting next to her on the plane had seen my mother's hands, full of pus, cracked and bleeding. She said she knew someone who could cure my mother, "un curandero en la ciudad." We were standing in the airport of Mexico City and my mother said "la ciudad" like it was the size of a small neighborhood.

For several years, Elvira's hands had been covered in a horrible rash. She had tried every kind of salve and ointment, Western medicine pills, homeopathy, and for some time she even went to an acupuncturist, but her hands would not heal.

As my parents stepped through the doors coming out of customs, I had seen Elvira scanning the crowd for her daughter's face. I often tried to spy my mother first in such meetings so I could catch her eyes catching mine, her face falling into relief and just . . . well, joy. I confess I milked those moments—to feel a mother's love.

At the time, I had been living in New York City for several years. Awaiting the publication of my first book of poetry and essays, I elected to finally make that long-awaited sojourn to México. I vainly fancied myself a kind of anonymous countryless writer as I boarded the plane for California to meet up with an old friend, Deborah, cross the border with her into Mexicali, and catch a train south into the Mexican heartland. My parents were to follow for a visit in a month's time. My plan: to return my mother's México back to her.

As Deborah and I arrived in Mexico City, not long after the election of Miguel de la Madrid Hurtado, the Mexican peso began to plummet. Little did even mexicanos know how suddenly and how permanently. For Deborah and me, it was as if overnight the value of our limited dollars made us, if not "ricas," certainly worry-free financially. So, before my parents' arrival, I got them a nice, but not fancy, hotel room in La Zona Rosa—a kind of hip, bohemian area with its pick of restaurants. This was before it "went gay."

During this period in my mother's life, my grandmother, well into her nineties, had become too fragile to live independently, even with a caretaker, so my mother took her into their home. Of all my mother's siblings, Elvira had been the only one to do so. The arrangement lasted no more than a year. Working an assembly line full-time and feeding a never-ending trail of visiting relatives constantly in and out of the house, while being the primary caretaker for her mother, was more than my mother could handle. The tíos and tías consulted and the decision was made to move my grandmother to a nursing home.

But Grama was not going to go down quietly. Her fierce obstinacy had molded her shrinking bones into the shape of skeletal ocotillo. Her family knew, without saying, she would soon be returning to the Sonoran Desert of her origins. Once she was in a nursing home, her half dozen children visited her each and every day, my mom and Auntie Eva preparing her dishes, doing her laundry, bathing her; it was almost as much work as had she been at home. But at least the evenings were their own; but not really, not for my mother, in whom guilt lingered and stole her sleep. Somehow, she believed herself never enough para su madre exigente.

But there was something else. Elvira's longing for her only son, someone with whom there had been a bitter unspoken rupture; someone whose wife, twenty years into marriage, still held my mother in little regard. Elvira denied it, the life she had hoped for in the generous charge of her son. She dreamed of una familia in abundance—with grandchildren, like my sister's, who would sit by her side, hold her hand, and ask for her stories. Pero nada. No shared Christmases. No Thanksgivings. No Fourth of July or Mother's Day picnics with my brother's four children. No chismeando con la daughter-in-law and no offerings de consejo in the raising of those children.

Nothing Mexican for miles.

She was useless to her son, her hands so empty of his touch, of his children's golden silk strands beneath her fingers. In horror, she watched her hands curl into ravaged claws of want. And so she arrives in México with a napkin-inscribed prescription for a cure.

The only word I recognize in the smudged ink is *Coyoacán*.

"Sí, Mamá," I say, "pero Coyoacán es un lugar muy grande."

No matter, this is our first order of business.

Stepping out of the hotel, we get a taxi and hire the driver for the day. I get into the front seat, as my father, Deborah, and Elvira squeeze into the back. I show the driver the napkin address, which is no address at all really—just the name of a main boulevard that runs for miles, with no building number and simply the words *El Doctor* scrawled on it. The driver figures he'll take us to the central area of Coyoacán and we'll see where to go from there. I agree. As we draw near, I see that we are not so far from Frida Kahlo's house and I make a mental note to take my parents there during their week's stay.

We make a turn onto a quieter street, driving now at a walking pace for no other reason than my mother says to slow down. And then suddenly, "Pare aquí, por favor." The driver stops the car. We are at the corner of a small dead-end cobblestoned street.

"I think this is it," my mother says. I look back at Deborah. We both know that there is no *logical* reason to stop here. I am nervous when my mother insists that the driver leave us there, but we pay him and wave him on.

And there we are—strangers in a strange land. (Or so I thought.) The four of us standing in the middle of an unknown street, looking for an unknown healer, just blocks away from what was once the sixteenth-century home of our ancestral foremother, Malintzín Tenepal.

My mother leads the pack of us as we walk down the center of the street, sentineled on each side by colonial-era buildings, fortressed with huge wooden front doors. *What is Elvira looking for?* She grabs my hand as we cross to a building about halfway down the street. To me, it feels absolutely arbitrary. To my mother, it is as it is. We approach the door. I knock. A few times. There is no response and then just as I lift my knuckles for a last try, a small kind of speakeasy viewing panel within the massive door opens. A middle-aged woman's face appears from within.

"Sí?"

Nervously I begin to explain our pursuit of the nameless curandero. The woman cuts me off.

"Vuelvan a las dos." El Doctor would see us between two and

four p.m., she said. And then she shuts the panel on my stunned face. But my mother wasn't stunned. She knew she was right where she belonged.

The moment my parents had stepped off the plane, I witnessed an aspect of Elvira I had never seen before. In their one-week stay, she moved about the boulevards and back roads of the city as if it were a 1930s Tijuana. For all the stories my mother had told me of her life en el otro lado de la frontera, that young urban "Tijua-nensa" was not the MexicanAmerican mother I knew. She was fluent in a Spanish I had never fully heard, which put everyone at ease, from concierges to waiters to the elder indígenas who dragged their knees across the cobblestones to La Basilica de la Virgen de Guadalupe. *Elvira had walked with them*, her daily vernacular told them, as a once teenaged worker in the Agua Caliente and on the next morning, when her own knees would scrape the cobblestones at las indígenas' side.

With two hours to kill before the curandero would return, I decided to walk my parents over to Frida Kahlo's La Casa Azul. As we turn the corner onto Londres, I stop in my tracks. There is Frida Kahlo herself standing among a small circle of men—middle-aged bohemian types, beards and baggy pants. Remember, this is 1983, long before the remaking of Frida into a cultural icon, where her ubiquitous unibrow face would appear on shopping bags, socks, T-shirts, and as a regular feature in drag lookalike contests entre la jotería.

But there she is—the living figure in full Frida regalia: Te-huana dress with rebozo, her black hair mounted upon her head with flowers, she leaning into a cane at her hip for support. And then I get it, seeing the movie camera hoisted over the shoulder of one man, the mics and cables. "Oh, they're making a movie," I say. And sure enough, as we approach La Casa, we learn that the house is closed for the filming.

It wasn't until several years later that I realized that the Frida I saw standing on the corner of Londres and Ignacio Allende was the Mexican actress Ofelia Medina and the film was *Frida: Naturaleza viva* by the Mexican director Paul Leduc. Sitting in a San Francisco movie house, I immediately recognized Medina's face and was suddenly reminded of the strange coincidence that occurred on that trip with Elvira. The surrealism of seeing the living Frida just outside her Blue House in Coyoacán made as much sense as landing on an unnamed street in that same neighborhood, with a wrinkled napkin as guide, that would lead us to the very healer my mother had so desperately needed.

At two o'clock, we enter the waiting room of el curandero and add our name to the long list of people—gente de la comunidad, working people. The long wait en la sala of the doctor's office would allow me time to assess the situation. Between two open doorways, I can see a handsome young man who passes quietly and familiarly among the back rooms. A cat, equally lithe, follows in his footsteps. Another cat also appears and disappears, or is it the same cat reappearing? Images of cats abound—small statues on end tables and paintings, along with literature about Eastern mysticism and . . . more cats.

I pick up a pamphlet with a line drawing of a cat on its cover and notice that it is written by El Doctor. It tells the personal story of his own spiritual awakening. After years of practicing Hinduism, he finally makes the pilgrimage to India en route to a guru he has longed to know. He is met by a woman who directs him to the waiting room. He sits alone in the room. No one else enters, but there is a cat in the corner of the room. It watches him as he waits and waits and waits—hours upon hours. The waiting is interminable as the young man grows more and more impatient and even agitated in spite of years of meditation practice. He begins to doubt himself: Why has he made the journey—wasted time and money? What if the guru never shows up? What was he looking for?

And then the cat echoes the man's own thoughts: "What *are* you waiting for?" The cat speaks aloud in the room. "What do you imagine the guru can tell you that you do not already know?" It is a simple question and the only one worth asking; its answer already resides in the body of the seeker. And with that, the young doctor packs it up and returns home to begin his healing practice in Mexico City.

When we enter the curandero's office, he and the young man I had seen earlier have a brief exchange. My mother and I both recognize the quality of their intimacy. She will say later, "Él es como tú." This is clearly no white-coat doctor. He wears comfortable clothes and is assisted by his gay lover in an open people's clinic where cats abound. He sits behind a wide carved wooden desk. We—my mother, Deborah, and I—occupy the other side. My dad is satisfied to remain in the waiting room.

Within minutes my mother will confess all that ails her. She pulls off the cotton gloves she wears to expose the landscape of her lament. It is my brother. It is her mother. It is a husband who cannot respond to her. And his "Entiendo, señora" may be all she needed to hear to lay down the burden of her sorrow. He touches her hands, fingers the crevices of her cracked wounds. They bleed lightly as he presses in, massaging and opening, dragging his thumb along the surface of her swollen and broken skin.

It takes only a few minutes. He tells her that she has to let go of the sorrow. Really, that's all he says. He reaches for a shelf and hands her a pint-size bottle of a clear liquid that looks like plain water. He instructs her on how to apply it to her wounds. He writes a prescription and directs me to the herbal pharmacy nearby. There will be tinctures of herbs and other remedies to pick up.

But my mother's hands seem to have already begun to heal, even before we exit through the giant wood door and out into the Coyoacán afternoon light. Elvira will soon run out of the bottled water and the tinctures, but she would not run out of the medicine the good doctor had provided. Miraculously, her hands (if not her heart) would remain healed for the rest of her life.

The next day, Deborah returned to California, boarding a plane home; and, as planned, I would have my parents all to myself. Our month of travel together hadn't been easy on Deborah's and my friendship. Since my move to the Northeast in 1980, I had become fully immersed, personally and politically, in its latinidad. In the context of México, Deborah's cultural whiteness shed light on my own vehement rejection of it. And, I suspect, I had not been so nice about it. Still, our friendship would survive this and the many years of change ahead of us.

The night before my parents' return to California, my mother and I sat at a piano bar late into the night, my dad dozing off— full of gin and the day's fatigue. Elvira spoke of her longing for the México of her past in a way I had never quite heard. She admitted that in 1939, she had not wanted to return to the Anglo world of the U.S. It seemed this short stay in La Ciudad de México had stirred up feelings she had long ago suppressed upon leaving Tijuana. Or perhaps it was the *quality* of our conversation, because for the first time in our lives we spoke to each other in an uninterrupted Spanish. Or maybe I was just queer and finally grown enough to understand that desire breaks rules as it breaks hearts.

Nothing México couldn't cure, I thought.

In the weeks that followed, I found myself alone and holed up in a small, more affordable hotel in another part of town. I was tired of traveling and there was so much to think about. One morning, a postal package was delivered to my room. I already knew its contents, but I had not been expecting the delivery so soon.

I open the brown wrapping. I observe the book's mauve and gold Aztec design, running my fingers over its title, subtitle, my name printed in bold caps. I turn the book over to see my own earnest face staring back at me. And with that, I prop myself up on that springy hotel bed in a dispassionate Mexico City and read *Loving in the War Years*, word by word, line by line, and page by page, stopping again and again on that paradoxical glyph of words: "Chicana Lesbian."

It was 1983 and I had never, in my life, read those two words as the subject of a book.

"Lo que nunca pasó por sus labios." *What have I done?*

My next trip to México would be two summers later. This time I traveled alone, at times dangerously, at times meeting up with friends. In the last weeks of my two-month stay, skirting the possibility of running into the young man with whom I had had a confused sexual encounter the previous night, I boarded a dawn bus from the then quiet seaside town of Zihuatanejo to Mexico City. A three-hundred-mile bus ride, on which I suddenly became so ill and progressively sicker as the miles blurred past me in a haze of fever.

I landed in the same no-frills hotel that I had stayed in two years earlier. (Within a month, it would be destroyed by the 1985 earthquake.) This time I arrived with a raging temperature, and within hours, I was shivering in sheets soaked with sweat. I was so sick that even the housekeeper, fresh sábanas in her arms, brought me manzanilla tea and worried over my condition. "¿No quiere ver a un doctor?" But physically I'd get over it—the fear in my gut was another question.

I was such a long way from home, México reminded me, in a Spanish I struggled to perfect; masked in a light-skinned face that betrayed my loyalties to a country of which I longed membership but held no right to. How I wanted to blend in as one of them. But I was not one of them and I was not gringa, but something/someone other than either. This is what brought the fever to the surface of my skin: the trepidation that who I was would never find home again.

Ten days later, regaining my strength, I decided to make my way down to el zócalo to attend a gathering to which I had been invited. Cuarto Creciente, a women's cultural center, stood just blocks away from where the huge stone disk of Coyolxauhqui, the Moon Goddess of the Mexica (Aztec) pantheon, was uncovered by electrical workers in 1978. Its discovery would lead to the full excavation of the Templo Mayor of Tenochtitlan.

What *I* discovered at Cuarto Creciente was a feminism that mirrored the cultural politics and racial and class biases of the white women's movement I had abandoned in the late seventies. Disoriented, I made my way through the labyrinth of those sixteenth-century walls, looking for a place to collect myself. And then I see her: a short brown-skinned woman standing at a window, looking out at the vast zócalo plaza. Her black hair hangs to her waist, she wears a huipil.

Again, I am disoriented. In my few visits to México, I quickly came to learn that most mexicanas do not wear Native huipiles unless they are bona fide members of an Indigenous pueblo or bourgeois artist types à la Frida. This woman was neither, I knew the second she turned around. "Hi, Cherríe," she says. It is that unmistakable chola California Chicana inflection. Her voice ran through me, a fire hot enough to melt me.

We had met before briefly, five years earlier, distant queer "cousin" poets and graduate students at San Francisco State. "Cousin" would be absolutely the wrong woman for me, but she was the right sex that night in my hotel room, to heal my fevered wounds. By morning I knew I had to get back home to California; not *to* her, but *through* her. An admission I made to no one, not even to myself.

TRAINING GROUND

We had a vision as women of color. What joined us was the Black in us, the Native and immigrant in us, the displaced, misplaced, lower caste, and castoff in us; the original bottom rung of a ladder that leads us up into transcendent meaning in the desire to converge across borders of once separation. This was the foundation of *This Bridge Called My Back: Writings by Radical Women of Color* in 1981.

In 1980, in search of a publisher for *Bridge*, the feminist anthology I coedited with Gloria Anzaldúa, I traveled east of the Mississippi for the first time in my life. Within months of that journey, I would move from San Francisco—first to Boston and then to New York City—and become completely ensconced in those cities' woman of color movements. Within a year, we were to grow a collective of women in the formation of Kitchen Table Women of Color Press. The mentorship I received from two of its founders, the bravest and most public Black lesbian writers of our time—Audre Lorde and Barbara Smith—will never be forgotten.

They provided the training ground for the Chicana Feminism I brought back with me to California.

Living in New York in the early 1980s, three thousand miles away from my Chicano community, at a time when the city's Chicano population was found in a small pocket of affirmative action students at Columbia, I often felt I was the only Chicana in the world to hold such a privileged position: to discover through political and cultural organizing what it meant to be a lesbian of color; to be uncompromised in every aspect of our identities; but also to learn to strategize politically about which foot to put forward first and when and where.

I loved that era of women of color feminism in New York: the late Sandra Camacho and I as co-coordinators/co-conspirators at New York Women Against Rape; working with those sisters at D.C.'s Rape Crisis Center to organize the first national conference of Violence Against Women of Color in 1982; dancing (lots of dancing), and drinking just enough to end up making out in the rain with that forbidden Nuyorican sister you wanted like a heartache, just before catching the subway back home to the girlfriend in Brooklyn.

I loved the Black Performance Poetry group—Gap Tooth Girlfriends—with Jewelle Gomez; and there was sister Alexis De Veaux's literary salons in Brooklyn where dreads and beauty and brilliance were unsurpassed; the truth-teller poet Cheryl Clarke was there, too; and, my sweetest love, Vienna Carroll, who after her day job at the Reproductive Rights National Network would sing a fluid jazz backup to Sapphire reading poetry at that Village bar into the midnight hour.

It was a grand New York life . . . but it was not home. Mi Chicanidad remained a remote and foreign location, like Native América, residing somewhere in the backcountry of the political and literary map of New York and the entire Northeast. México had shown me that. The harder work was to go home. And it was impossible to explain this to anyone who asked, especially to those African American sisters who had been my teachers and lovers; to Vienna, one of the happiest periods of my life. And I was leaving her.

I left to go back to California to be Chicana. And I was not so well versed at it. Because you really do just have to, plain and simple, practice what you preach. And, for me, as a writer, the preaching *was* the practice. The truth was I was afraid to love a Mexican woman, to suffer her cruelties, as I had my own mother's. I did not believe I would survive it. I went anyway.

OLD SCHOOL

The thick velvet stage curtain is slowly drawn open by the back of a hand, and a figure with an equally thick curtain of black hair emerges through it. She is someone with such a steady lightness of being, such contained and complex beauty, it will take me several years to find the resolve to press my mouth to hers in a kiss I know will mean a marriage vow.

I had been expecting her. We had spoken by phone a month earlier in San Francisco. It was 1992—a planned meeting of shared interests as artists, arranged by shared friends. Celia was originally from Sacramento, California, then working in Chicago, and I had come to Chicago to work on my play *Shadow of a Man*. The venue was an old retired firehouse, transformed into a theater space by Chicano ingenuity. Perhaps it was also Chicano ingenuity that had brought Celia and me together.

We have lunch. Celia's gaze meets mine, unafraid, effortless. The attraction is mutual and evident. Her openness stuns me. Nothing is being "worked." She is just simply present. She has a girlfriend, as do I, mine a feminist arts organizer, with whom I share a home in San Francisco. Celia and I spend the day together. Her girlfriend even joins us for a drink before taking off, her dignity intact. We go out with the gay boys, my hosts, to a blues club; and then she invites me back to her home.

Celia makes me a bed on the living room couch. Perfectly made, fresh sheets, home-sewn pillowcases. She tucks me in, kissing me sisterly but she is no sister. Before the couch moment, she had shared the two things that seemed to matter most to her, a painting and a plant. She tells me about the painting, *Interrupted Fertility*. Its earth-colored waters are brushed onto three panels of amate paper pressed against weathered wood. A Mesoamerican Quetzalcoatl serpent lies across the panels, severed at its middle. Next to her painting, la pejuta grows in a small pot. I do not know what to look for in its flower shape, how each cactus huddles one against the other for protection. I only read its meaning to her— in the way she offers me to gaze upon it like a god.

She does not mention her children.

In 1993, Celia would return to Northern California to re-collect the splintered lives of her adult children, some with several children of their own. In that same year, I would give birth to Rafael Ángel, in what had become a long-term relationship with my partner and in friendship with my son's father, a younger queer Chicano writer. Those are the large facts. The stories of those breakups and reunions among lovers and children are written elsewhere, if only as scarred etchings along the banks of my memory. But the truest story is this: *I almost lost my son at birth. And that changed everything.*

At the age of forty, I became pregnant upon my first attempt at a home-based insemination. I had never been pregnant before and the ease with which my pregnancy occurred bespoke a spirit eagerly awaiting its time on this planet. As did my son's premature birth.

In late June, while I was visiting my parents in San Gabriel, my water broke, a full three months before my due date. I was rushed to Kaiser Hospital in Hollywood, where, one week later, Rafael Ángel emerged in natural childbirth, weighing just two and a half pounds. Although born so small, my baby was relatively healthy, with strong lungs and a fierce will. Once stabilized, and after ten days at Hollywood Kaiser, Rafaelito was transported back to San Francisco and to its Kaiser Neonatal nursery.

Within a matter of days, however, he contracted a life-threatening intestinal infection fairly common among preemies. As was the case with Rafaelito, it can overwhelm a small infant at an alarmingly rapid pace. In the three and a half months that my newborn son would remain in the hospital, he would undergo two surgeries, both of which put his life in question.

As they did mine.

For I would never be the same after that . . . after watching my child in his Isolette being pushed through the surgery doors, my heart in a vise of panic and dread. Suddenly, Rafaelito lifts his palm-sized head up and around to look back at me.

Mamá, are you still there? his eyes ask.

My eyes meet his.

Sí. Siempre.

And the doors close after him.

The endless two hours in the surgery waiting room felt strangely familiar. The helplessness with which I entreated my diosas—obsessively running through my mind promises and prayers, stacking up useless bargaining chips prompted by pure fear—was no different than my childhood scratching scratching scratching to ward off my mother's death. But as this new terror arose, thrashing against the wall of my chest, so close to bursting, I suddenly realized I was no longer a child, but the *mother* of a child, who desperately needed me to be wholly present at that moment. There was no "god" in such fear.

And so . . . somehow . . . finally . . . I just let go . . .

I hear myself echoing my mother's words aloud, words she would repeat each time she entreated her santos, lighting la veladora on her altar. *If it is God's will . . . con el favor de Dios.* We can control very little in this life, she knew, much better than I. And ultimately, we *are* in "god's" hands.

Waiting outside that surgery, twenty-three years ago, I finally understood: my son *was* in those same godly hands, and I only prayed that the surgeon's hands would be guided by them, by *my* god—the benevolent wisdom of the universe; a spirit calling, a reason for us to be here for the long and short of our lives. Then, within minutes of my surrender, the nurse from surgery comes into the waiting room. "Your baby is going to be fine," she says.

How *do* we come to know the meaning of our impermanence if not through the (almost) loss of those dearest to us? I thank my son for this lesson, as I will thank my mother, twelve years down the road.

I would walk alone or I would walk with she who could walk fearlessly in the face of death.

In the fall following Rafaelito's fourth birthday and just as I began to release myself from the profound susto of the near loss of him, I invited Celia on our first official date after five years of friendship. Sitting at what would become our favorite neighborhood Italian restaurant in Oakland, I suddenly recognized that all I needed in a woman sat across that tea-candle-lit table. And Celia talked on and on and I was not listening, only finally allowing my return to the love of a Mexican woman in my life.

There had been other Chicanas before Celia—other Latinas, women who taught me brutal, naked, and luminous lessons about the measure of my own desires. There was the woman nearly twenty years older, una puertorriqueña whom I made love with briefly and have loved eternally, who left me hungrier for the brevity of the taste of her. "Brevity" could also be said of the life of la mestiza indígena with the leather hands of a sculptor touching mine. *The last of her was a gray ash dust, pressed palm into palm, into woman-palm.* There was "the hungry woman," whose young son first schooled me in the freedom of loving not as a dutiful daughter, but as an almost-mother, where one's own needs came so spontaneously second.

The footpath I walked leading up to Celia's open heart was paved with the cruelties of women, including my own unsparing acts. Mexican women could break me, my history told me, because they mattered to me that much. Gazing across the restaurant table, upon Celia's animated face, I think—*Maybe with this one, it will be different.*

From the early loss of her mother, through teen pregnancy, to the rough red road of raising children as a single lesbian mother, Celia's aspirations for a restored familia mirrored my own longing. Celia's values had been garnered from la palabra y práctica of the Ódami Mexican grandmother who raised her. Domitila and Elvira, as mexicanas of the same generation, unwittingly provided us with common ethics upon which to construct our queer familia.

With Celia's eight-year-old granddaughter, Camerina, and my Rafael Ángel in tow, we landed upon that first rise of foothill overlooking the Fruitvale barrio and made Oakland, California, our home. Together, at the age of forty-five, she and I began to walk a road of contested mothering wherein the only guidepost was the steadfast example of the two old-school Mexican mothers who had preceded us.

By the time my mother is diagnosed with Alzheimer's at the close of 2003, another grandchild of Celia's is gestating her way into our home and hearts. Cetanzi would be the first to call me Abuelita.

A ROLLING STONE

There were times in which I did not know whether my mother was truly demented or just Mexican in a white world. I knew she was ill, that she suffered enormously; but I often doubted if the medicine for that illness (psychotropic drugs and the culture of care for elders in this country) was adequately designed for the woman whose emotional memory defied the limits and logic of occidental plotlines. Was it designed for an eighty-six-year-old woman who, even in her so-called dementia, could not forget the past, who believed in the dead and knew they came to visit with messages truer than the dreary sound bites of consumer culture?

What *I* remember is the fall from the curb in the shopping mall. Nothing major, only a slip of the foot. My mother had been looking elsewhere, her eyes scanning the parking lot through the hazy Valley smog for my father's navy-blue sedan. The doctors concurred: "a slight concussion, nothing major." Yes, there was the scarring in the brain and some shrinkage had begun. "Perfectly normal for her age." But something in my mother began to shift that day, something so subtle, so certain.

On that day my mother began to leave us.

Everything about our upbringing as MexicanAmerican children revered our elders. With elders, we learned to offer a glass of water, a cup of coffee, the last empty chair in a room. We extended our arm for them to hold as they crossed a street, got out of a car, stepped into a bathtub. With elders, we learned to refrain from comment when we disagreed, endured long hours of visita without asking to eat, and never refused what was offered to us, no matter how stale the saltines. With elders, we also learned that if we made ourselves invisible enough, they might forget we were there and reveal all: stories with the power to conjure a past as stained and gray with intrigue as the aging photographs that held them.

As the century turned and my mother entered her mid-eighties, my sister and I began to warily approach the subject of my mother's failing memory—to each other, to our father, and to her surviving younger sister and brother. "It's normal," everyone kept telling us. For a year or so prior, this had been my refrain as well, against my sister's entreaties for "getting our mom some real help." For it was JoAnn who lived within a half hour's drive of our childhood home in San Gabriel. It was also my sister who endured my mother's virulent denial about missed appointments, burned pots, forgotten phone conversations, lost keys and twenty-dollar bills, and seemingly delusional suspicions about our family's treatment of her.

"Your sister hasn't called me in weeks," she'd complain to me over the phone in Oakland. "I don't think I've even seen her in a month or more."

I would call JoAnn to urge her to visit.

"I just saw her on Monday, brought them hamburgers. She's forgotten." What wrenched my heart the most was the futility of my sister's actions. My mother suffered from "not-seeing" her because she could not remember. What she did remember was the nameless feeling of missing someone or something. Was it her un-remembered self?

She was waning. Her world was becoming more insular. True, up to the last days of her life, Elvira would continue to ex-hibit great shows of affection when inspired, but slowly she began to pull away from us and into the world of her own preoccupa-tions. This is not uncommon for elders where the physical require-ments of aging often mandate their full attention. But in my mother's case, that seemingly benign fall in the Montebello Mall initiated an entrenched self-absorption, thrusting her and her family into years of increasing agitation and dis-ease. My mother had never been an easygoing person, but gradually as her atten-tion to what had been the normal routines of her life began to fade—cooking, cleaning, conducting familial relations—Elvira fell into great bouts of depression and fury.

Elders were to be honored at all costs; but when was the cost too high? We had given wide berth to the pure will and visceral knowing that defined my mother for most of our lives; this is, after all, what saved us. So how could we suddenly require her to sur-render her will to us?

My mother's eighty-sixth birthday marked a turning point for me when I began to loosen the hold on my conviction that my mother's *fuerza* was enduring. On the night of her celebration at a nearby old-style Bavarian restaurant, which catered to elders of all kinds, my mother had opened a full table of gifts and responded to each present with perhaps a bit too much exuberance; this, no doubt, the result of the amount of wine she had drunk that evening. But the following morning, suspecting Elvira hadn't been all there the previous night, I asked her if she would like to see her presents. *What?* She didn't remember getting presents. I brought out the pile of opened boxes, the tongues of white tissue hanging out from their mouths. She was elated at the sight of so many gifts. And so Elvira celebrated her birthday all over again for the first time. That was a good day, a day I could pretend *not* remembering was really due to the wine and normal for an eighty-six-year-old and it isn't called Alzheimer's and it won't get worse, because that day of *not* remembering made Elvira happy. In my heart, I knew differently.

Three months later, I arrive back home again in San Gabriel for a visit. It is not yet spring, but still a warming midafternoon. I expect to find my mother in her daily routine: scrubbing a pot here, folding a sweater there; walking from room to room, opening and shutting drawers and cupboards; transporting handfuls of clothing from one spot to another and back again. My father would have already spent a good part of the day in his office, a kind of makeshift construction of swelling fake wood panels, pressed against the crumbling stucco walls of the garage.

I enter the TV room (my childhood bedroom) and spy my mother, her head dropped back against the couch, her mouth open. She is so drugged that she isn't even snoring. This is not the first time I have found her this way. I rush out to my dad's office.

Since his retirement from the railroad freight yards, he had cultivated a steady stream of clients doing tax returns. Even during the off-season, he would manage to find much to do. Away from my mother's purview, he submitted quarterly reports, worked on occasional audits, and ordered sports books and big-band music videos.

I interrogate him: How many pills is she taking? Let me see the prescription bottles. Hurried and nervous, he mumbles shamed inaudible responses as he hobbles with his walker back into the house. We rummage through the kitchen cupboards; the pills are everywhere, half-filled, refilled, there is no rhyme or reason to the amounts. "She gets up in the middle of the night." He stammers, "I . . . I don't know what she's taking."

Right away, I am on the phone to my sister. She tracks down my mother's doctor, who, unbeknownst to JoAnn, has given our mother drugs for depression. JoAnn and I soon dump the doctor when, during the quickly scheduled visit, he tries to assess my mother's memory loss by having her remember the line "A rolling stone gathers no moss," a sentence that means nothing to my unlettered Mexican mother. "Pendejo," JoAnn and I agree about the doctor.

It is sometimes no more complicated than this: there are culturally stupid and lazy doctors who see elders as useless annoyances to be pacified with antidepressants. All the while our elders' actions tell us the opposite; that they are not stupid, but suffering a deep inarticulate loss, about which they do not have the confidence to share, even with their most beloved. These old ones are holding their cards very close to their chest. They've been dealt a bad hand. They are bluffing and everyone knows it.

JoAnn finds my mother a gerontologist, a psychiatrist, and a social worker within a week. Her thirty-plus years of working in the public school system, first as an elementary school teacher and then as a principal, where children are often last on the political agenda, taught my sister how to be an advocate and work that system for those who cannot. It may be what my sister is best at: the battlefield of social welfare and justice—its black-and-white clarity, while the front lines of personal relationships are so much more difficult to negotiate.

Getting my mother to a doctor's visit was seldom challenging. Elvira loved to be doted on by male doctors, especially handsome forty-something Asian American ones, which aptly described her new personal physician, who commented on how her fierceness and fine features reminded him of his own mother. In fact, Elvira flirted with doctors who catered to her. Although at times encouraging my mother's flirtations served as an effective strategy for getting her to open up to her physicians, the game thinly cloaked her desperate attempt at control. Her disabling vulnerability teetered dangerously on the other edge of that coquettish smile, and the best of doctors could spot it. Her daughters feared and begged for her face to fall. Elvira needed help.

A week later, my sister, mother, and father sit in the psychiatrist's office. The doctor, a white man, wears a suit and sits behind a desk. My sister is grateful for this, hoping that without the telltale signs of a doctor, my mother might be tricked into answering questions she would otherwise reject. But the underlying tension is palpable: my mother fully suspects betrayal by her eldest daughter and husband at every turn. In my mother's mind, the two are co-conspirators, plotting her submission to a culturally alien healthcare system intent on her demise. These are not her words, but it *is* her conviction.

The meeting with the psychiatrist goes smoothly enough until he asks my mother directly, "Your husband and daughter are concerned about your loss of memory. Have you noticed that you have been forgetting things?" And that's all it takes.

After several years of the most blatant examples of my mother's slipping hold on her own daily story—the inability to even eat a plate of food not buried under a hill of salt because she'd forgotten she had salted it only moments before—the doctor's question throws Elvira into a frenzy of fury. He, too, is in collusion with these traitors, trying to ridicule and humiliate her. She bolts out of his office and into the reception area in a tirade of curses. In a way this was the best move my mother could have made since she had grown so expert at "keeping face" with the experts.

Stunned, the psychiatrist asks, "Does she often explode like this?"

"Yes," JoAnn replies.

"She's clearly bipolar. How long has this been going on?"

And JoAnn had to laugh to herself at the psychiatrist's on-the-spot diagnosis. "We've lived with this all of our lives," JoAnn answers. "It's only more aggravated now."

I, too, laugh when my sister recounts this conversation and the entire episode on the phone to me later that evening. My mother's intractability was as connected to her as sinew to muscle. It was, in fact, the very muscle of control that she had always held over her family. Her anger, and our fear of it, kept us in line as best a single mother (for Elvira felt herself alone in the rearing of her children) could.

Shaking hands with the psychiatrist, my father and sister exit his office only to discover my mother is not waiting for them outside the door. They fully believed that once inside the waiting room she would've recovered herself to save face.

"Does she wander?" the receptionist asks.

"No," JoAnn answers, and does not add the truer statement, *but she bolts to save her life.*

My father and JoAnn hurry out of the medical building in search of my mother. My sister eventually finds her crouched behind a bush across the parking lot. From there, she was able to see her daughter and husband come out of the building. She could watch them search for her, never losing sight of them. My mother never once put herself in danger. That much control she still had.

The senior-care social worker turned out to be "una americana, a nice lady" who came to visit her. Vera seemed agreeable enough even when she had to do tests about which JoAnn and I had alerted the "nice lady" in advance. We wanted our mother's memory assessed, not her education level, averting any situation that might shame our mother about her lack of schooling. There was no surprise when the social worker concluded, "Your mother needs care. She shouldn't be left alone too much." At this, my father drops his eyes, knowing he had endured my mother's outbursts by sequestering himself in his garage office for long hours of the day.

So we agreed (at least in theory) to bring in an attendant to help with the cooking, the shopping, and some light housecleaning. She would monitor my mother's meds and, no doubt, provide her with a little extra much-needed company. We had not consulted with my mother about this in advance, fearing that if she knew too soon, she would wear us down with resistance.

Days later, the attendant showed up for an interview and I was forced to tell my mother why she had come. My mother was incensed, of course, feeling that her last hold on the integrity of her home was dissolving before her eyes. She would barely talk to the woman, who did little to ingratiate herself to my mother. Maybe that was just what Elvira needed—a no-nonsense MexicanAmerican woman, whom my mom could not manipulate. These are the stories we tell ourselves to justify decisions riddled with doubt. The other more traditional "señoras" we had previously hired to help out around the house were regularly sent away by my mother after a cup of reheated coffee and a few stale cookies from the cupboard.

"No, todo 'stá bien. No necesitamos nada."

They, too, knew better than to challenge the dictums of their elders.

It was all arranged. Starting Monday, the attendant would begin to take care of my mother during the weekdays. Vera threatened to pack her bags. And so we pumped up our dad. "You gotta be brave," we told him. But our father was not brave and when the attendant arrived that Monday morning, he predictably yielded to his wife's threats and sent her away.

What we didn't know was that the day before, our brother had shown up from out of state. Even when James lived within a few hours' drive of my parents, he seldom visited them for longer than an evening, separated by long periods of absence. For the most part, his visits and communications numbered no more than two times a year, a restaurant meal squeezed between business meetings and golf rounds. Possibly for AngloAmerican families, this was acceptable; but for our extended familia mexicana, his distance remained, for all of us, completely incomprehensible.

"Cleave to your wife," my brother's trusted spiritual adviser, the monsignor, an elderly Irishman, had counseled, quoting Genesis. And with that, James settled on the outside what could never be resolved internally, the forty-year antagonism between his wife and his mother and sisters.

It had started as early as the age of sixteen, when James began dating an attractive and strong-minded "American" girl from our high school. Entering la familia Moraga was no doubt a culture shock for young Aileen. We all watched in stunned amazement when the things we took for granted in our home and that were loved by so many of our Mexican and non-Mexican friends alike were challenged aloud by the teenager. She didn't understand why James was required to kiss his mother and father and two teenaged sisters and abundant aunts and uncles each time he entered or left the house. It eluded her why an older brother might genuinely *want* to spend some time in his younger sisters' company, if only to bang on the guitar and sing silly folk songs. She ignored the presumption that after months became years into their relationship she might offer to set a table or pick up a dish after dinner. The hardest part was that she made little effort to know our mother or, as Elvira put it, *to leave the boy's lap long enough to talk to [her], even if it was just pretend and she didn't really give a damn about la vieja.*

The last bit was just one line from our mother's litany of discontent, spoken behind closed doors each time her son left the house, girlfriend in tow. The receding sound of tires against gravel was our cue to speak once James had maneuvered our family '65 Chevy down the narrow driveway and out into the wider American world of awaiting promise.

In the beginning, our family remained in a kind of holding pattern in the young couple's presence. What had worked so beautifully in public—the Student Body President/Captain of the Football Team going steady with the Cheerleader/Homecoming Queen—proved to be a miserable failure at home. We dashed and darted around the censored subject of the ill-fitting familial match, the silence growing increasingly strained and hostile.

My mother decreed that we were never to address the matter directly with our brother. As a result, Sunday dinner-table conversations were painful exercises in suppression, where Aileen freely expressed her right-wing political views about abortion and all those *MexicanAmericans who had suddenly turned Chicano,* not to mention those *un-American antiwar hippie protesters.* Meanwhile, my mother would cut her eyes at us, a knife blade of censure flung across the dining room table, to silence me and my sister. I swallowed my rice and beans, along with my resentment, and lined up the toothpicks extracted from my taquitos like little foot soldiers along my plate: my own private 1968 army of dissent.

Aileen was entitled to her position because she was James's girlfriend, but also because she was "American" in a way that we, as *Mexican*Americans, were not, especially my mother. Aileen was not *required* to know us culturally. We did not feel similarly entitled.

My father had nothing to say on the subject.

One day, unexpectedly, James decided to leave Aileen. By then, away at college, all he said was that she had been his only steady girlfriend and, well . . . they were both Catholics and, well . . . as my mother intimated, *a young man has feelings*. (The implication, of course, was that a young woman does not; and that the young man might need to go explore those "feelings" with other women first. All Elvira's perspective.)

JoAnn and I couldn't contain our excitement over the prospect of a free life for our brother, one that might lead him to a kind-hearted girl who might even love his family, too. I see now how much we perceived my brother's choices through the prism of our own lives. James was the master of his own destiny. As females we would never know such freedom. Yet, culturally speaking, he was emotionally tethered to a Mexican family of women that had a direct stake in his choices. Perhaps the very onus of this was why my brother chose to leave us.

Suddenly, Aileen wants that long-awaited conversation with the much-maligned mother. One afternoon, she spills into our house crying, *I love him. Convince him to take me back. Please, Mrs. V.* And Mrs. V will do just that. At last, a player in her son's life.

A few days later, James is home for the weekend, kicking back in his Bermuda shorts on the living room La-Z-Boy, watching TV. The late-morning sun pours through the sheer curtains. Elvira enters, sits down on the carpet at her son's feet. She puts her hand on the naked part of his thigh just above the well-muscled knee-cap, and tells him in plain words that she knows what he's feeling.

"It's only natural," she says.

My mother would retell this story over and over again. It captured a brief moment in time when her word mattered in the life of her only son. But, more than this, it was a conversation about desire. This is what seemed to matter most to Elvira; that she knew the world of men's desire well enough to advise him, even as it conflicted with the unbending Irish Catholic education we learned in our mission schools. My mother was well versed in the real rules of the world but was seldom asked to draw on them in guiding her son as he grew into American Christian manhood.

On that Bermuda shorts Saturday morning, my mother urged my brother to take Aileen back "because she is a good girl and would be a good mother for your children." And so James did take her back. And true to biblical teachings, he would "cleave" to her. And the soon-to-be wife quickly dumped her soon-to-be mother-in-law, who had supported her in her time of need.

And we daughters chide, "We told you so, Mom. Why didn't you just leave it alone?"

She responds, "Because I know how it is to love and be left like that."

I am nine years old. It is a Saturday chore day. I am vacuuming the hallway.

"I have something to tell you," my mother says over the blast of suction from the Kenmore. I catch the unease in her eyes and in the rope of dish towel she wrings at the waist of her apron. My heart quickens, and I hit the "off" switch with my sandaled toe.

"Yeah . . . ?"

"Mi'ja, I was married before your father."

They had met during the war, she says. And that's about all she says. I am relieved to learn there were no other children, relieved to

*put a name and a story to the stranger's portrait, foreign and blond,
that lay at the thinning bottom of the red-and-white May Company
box in the cupboard.*

Many years later my mother revealed that she was the one who
decided to divorce when she learned that her husband had reen-
listed after the war. "It was so he could have other women," she
said. *Too many women in too many ports* is how I remember it.

Once in the early years of James's marriage, my mother came to
my sister and me and asked us to write his wife a letter. She
wanted to explain her feelings, she said. "If I have ever done anything to offend you . . ." was the line I remember most as she
dictated the words to us. I also remember my mother's utter
shock to receive a letter back from her daughter-in-law, whose single response was "Examine your conscience," refusing any gesture
of reconciliation. The courage it took for my mother to swallow her
pride in order to "write" the letter was just one measure of her
love for her son. Perhaps it was the depth of this love that was so
hard for Aileen. We would never know.

Elvira is anxious. *There is always so much to do. Is it lunchtime? Have
we eaten?* She goes to the kitchen, opens the refrigerator, and takes
out half a tuna sandwich brought home from the coffee shop three
days earlier, and puts it onto a plate for her husband. She sits and
waits. She rises, goes to a kitchen drawer, removes a pile of unopened mailers, and crosses to her bedroom. She puts the mailers
into a shoebox at the base of the closet. She returns to the kitchen,
takes the coffee grounds from the pot of cold coffee on the stove,
and dumps them into a mound on the pantry shelf. She shuts the
cupboard. She sits again and waits. He'll want coffee. She goes to

the stove and turns on the near-empty coffee pot to high. She goes outside to call him in. The sun is setting into a hot muggy pink sky. She takes the hose to water her plants. The hose gets heavier every day. She hears men's voices through the garage walls.

On the Sunday before the attendant's scheduled arrival, my father escorts his son into his office, out of Vera's earshot. There he confides the weight of his troubles—his volatile wife, his demanding daughters, his barely functioning but "I can manage" hips. When the subject of the attendant comes up, my brother responds, "Don't listen to my sisters. She's your wife. Do whatever you think is best."

James gave this advice after assessing our mother's condition over one meal; a meal during which Elvira put on that same coquettish face she had for the stranger-doctors. I had observed this for much of my adult life. As James grew more estranged, my mother grew stranger in her manner toward him.

On the few occasions when he visited without his wife, Vera seemed to "perform" herself. Once at an Easter meal, I watched as my mother twisted a full ninety degrees to talk with her son sitting next to her, literally turning her back on the rest of the family for the entire two-hour length of the dinner. She leaned into him like a lover, her makeup gleaming. When her son entered a room, all others were eclipsed and all was forgiven, or so she pretended. When she could still remember to pretend.

During that garage meeting, James also encouraged my dad to continue to postpone hip surgery if that was what he chose. When my father justified his inaction with "Your brother agreed," there was no mistaking the bitterness in my sister's and my responses. James had never endured the smell of urine on my father's pants or the rank odor heat-baked into the broken upholstery of the driver's seat of his car. My brother had no way of knowing my father's real condition because he was never around long enough to observe that his father's deteriorated hips couldn't get him to the bathroom fast enough nor allow him to bend sufficiently to wipe well once he got there. He didn't see him take a full five minutes to roll out of the driver's seat of the car nor recognize his complete inability to move quickly enough to come to my mother's aid.

In retrospect, the failed attempt at home care for my mother probably went the way it was supposed to. My mother's fierce opposition and the stalemate of fear and resentment that was the fabric of my parents' marriage may not have allowed for any other course of action. In this sense, my brother was blameless, constructing his advice on a fantasy marriage where the husband is not afraid of becoming an orphan and can monitor his wife's well-being with the confidence of an endowed knowing. Perhaps my brother needed his illusions about his father, in spite of evidence to the contrary.

My brother's authority, as the eldest and a male, went unchallenged within our family. In this respect, James remained inextricably Mexican; for it was my mother who had crafted my brother into the role of patriarch, the same role her elder brother and father had occupied in her own life. His long absences notwithstanding, my brother's word was law. In all other aspects of our cultura, James was, as he once described it, "just passing through."

LIKE THE HERON

We knew we had been functioning in the spirit of "last times" for a few years. Although the pretext was a family birthday, my mother's last trip to my home in Oakland signaled in many ways her final experience within the grander world outside of her home.

In their own house, my parents continued to cope in the best way possible, managing to construct a semblance of a life by simply responding to the requirements of aging: three meals a day, doctor's visits, and a decent night's sleep. My mom did her best to stay busy, clothed, and out of the way of the stove's flame. La familia came to visit, but less and less as my mother's forgetfulness meant hospitality was reduced to shorter and shorter present-tense sentences, sudden bouts of irritability, and a cup of reheated coffee. It seemed that our extended familia was shrinking in proportion to my mother's brain, as the disquiet in her heart grew beyond the possibility of remedy or respite.

My parents arrived at the Oakland airport peaceably enough in the late afternoon, under the watchful eye of my sister. We all returned back to my house to prepare the cena, allowing my mother a few small tasks that occupied her, drying a few dishes, slicing celery, etc. But after dinner ended, my mother grew anxious. She was tired and ready to go home. We reminded her that she was in Oakland and that they had flown in a plane to get here. She became irate. She had told my father not to give "that man" their car. I looked over to my sister confused. "She means the valet parking at the airport."

I smiled as I watched my mother cross to the kitchen, where Celia was washing pots. My mother approached her with her formal face, the one she used for people not related by blood. She appealed to Celia's good sense: "I am a very important businesswoman," she entreated her. "I've got a lot to take care of at home." Celia was compassionate, but unyielding. "Entiendo, señora, you can go home tomorrow," she said. My mother exited the kitchen, her fury building.

We, her family, watched in stunned silence as she moved about the house, desperately trying to figure a way out. The split-level hillside house confused her. She became increasingly disoriented, increasingly volatile. I stood up from the table, as all heads turned toward me. "I'll talk to her," I say. My sister's eyes locked with mine. This was how our tag team worked. She, the ardent crusader for my mother's health care; I, the caretaker of the heart.

My mother disappeared down the hallway. I followed, finding her at the foot of a half set of stairs leading to my office. I knew she had no idea where she was. "Mom," I try. She spins around and her look chills me. I am in her way, that's all she knows, an obstacle to the home, the bed, the familiarity, which even the face of her youngest daughter cannot provide. I am terrified; there is no other word for it. I outweigh my mother by at least forty pounds, but her rage completely immobilizes me. My mind races for a so-lution, a strategy. How do I stop her? Suddenly it comes to me, as a seduction of sorts. I feel myself literally growing into the com-passionate husband, the devoted eldest son, all the missing men in her life—the ones I know she will submit to, if only to be re-lieved once and for all of the burden of her own control. I feel my-self more man than ever before.

I hear my voice deepen. "You've got to stay, Mamá." It has dropped to a register I intuitively feel she might respond to.

"I'd rather take poison than stay," she spits back at me.

So it is war. I try again: "Well, I'm not giving you poison and you *are* staying."

Then, nada. No comeback. This is the opening. I go to her, put my arms around her, no longer man but lesbian daughter. Her body remains stiff but does not resist. I escort her downstairs and into Celia's and my bedroom. I remove her clothes and put on her pajamas, all the while speaking to her those small cariños I learned from her own mouth, the ones she showered me with as a child. I put her into bed and draw the clean sheets and comforter up around her neck. I kiss her forehead and lay her down to sleep. And she does sleep peacefully throughout the night.

In the morning, she is in good humor. Upon awakening, I had assumed we would put my parents on a plane that morning, but by 8 a.m., my mother's distress from the previous night is long forgotten. Hours later, I find myself walking with Elvira on a short flat trail surrounded by the sand dunes of Point Reyes Seashore, an hour's drive north of Oakland. My father, unable to walk any distance, sits with his walker at the edge of the parking lot, tak-ing in the view of sand dune and open blue sky. My sister has hiked with Rafa down to the seashore, their pant legs rolled up and ready for the frigid September waters.

En route to a lagoon nestled among the dunes, Elvira's step

at eighty-eight is as steady as a sixty-year-old's. I wrestle with the contradiction that my father, his mind intact, is unable to accompany us on this walk due to stubbornness and fear of hip surgery, while my mother's withering mind is housed in a body of enduring agility. I am grateful for this moment alone with her, as though last night's encounter in the hallway had earned us this intimacy.

A heron tips into the shallow waters.

"Mira, Mamá," I say.

She seems to take it all in—the long-necked elegance of the shorebird, the quiet green rippling of the lagoon, the limitless generosity of blue above us, the faded outline of the moon that floats inside it. The leather of my mother's palm clutches my hand—always the measure of her love. Like the heron, I drink in this liquid knowing—the permeability of the moment. Elvira had worked so damn hard for us and she was slipping away . . .

And then, without warning, la mujer que recuerdas como tu mamá returns to you with todo su ánimo. And you begin to forget the years of aggravated grief caused by the turmoil of her illness and you tell yourself, *She has come back to stay*. You begin to doubt the truth. You think it was only the wrong combination of medications; it was only that she drank too much wine; it was only that she was so tired; it was only the chronic pain from her arthritis; it was only my missing brother, my distracted father, my too-earnest sister . . .

But it was only a matter of time until the harsh fact of my mother's departure became undeniable.

THE MOTHER OF THE BRIDE

I always knew you didn't love him," my mother had announced to my sister when after twenty years and four children, JoAnn decided to divorce her first husband. Elvira applauded JoAnn's decision in the hopes that true love awaited. Ten years later, JoAnn wanted to convince her mother that love had in fact arrived.

Weren't the tall, kindly Anglo husband, the handsome adult sons who "gave her away," the tasteful cream-colored wedding dress, and the well-shaped middle-aged body that fit into it, meant as the ultimate romantic farewell for my mother? There was a certain logic to JoAnn's resolve in that she had fashioned many of her life choices in the hope of Elvira's favor. The fact that my mother's state of mind had recently become less and less predictable did not dissuade my sister. It only made the execution of the wedding plans more urgent, more driven.

"You over there!" the foreman shouted across the crowd of expectant faces. The women pressed up against the gates of the Los Angeles walnut

factory. It was 1939 and an assembly-line job was hard to come by in those times. Elvira had returned from Tijuana, jobless, with a widowed mother and siblings to support.

"He spotted me out of all the women."

My mother had told us the story many times.

"Me?" she asked.

Dressed in what remained of her Tijuana Salón de Oro attire, she could feel the bitter envy of the women around her.

"Yeah, you."

And the MexicanAmerican foreman offered her the job on the spot.

Romance for Elvira resided mostly in the story. She was a woman who knew not to appear desperate even in desperate times; who knew how to place a stylish hat on her head at such an angle that people spotted her in a crowd and offered her refuge. This is what distinguished a person: that knife-edge balance between humble circumstance and the pride of survival. "No matter how poor we were, we always had a clean tablecloth to sit down to."

Ironically, my sister's wedding did result in being about Elvira. True to form, my mother stole the show when at the reception she ended up knocked out on the dance floor. The groom had spun la delgadita Elvira around for a turn, let her hand slip from his, and she went flying. She hit her neatly coiffured head on the edge of the Mexican-tiled bar, and was down for the count.

Celia and I had been out on the balcony overlooking the man-made lake, a moon just beginning to form on the surface of the water. My eldest niece rushes out to find us. "Grandma's fallen!" We quickly wend our way through the crowd and I spy my mother, two bird legs sticking out of the circle of people hovering over her, her dancing shoes pointing straight up at perfect right angles. *The Wicked Witch of the West*, I can't help but think. The house of age and pure stubbornness has finally fallen on top of her. Or maybe it was my sister's stubbornness that came crashing down: her insistence on grabbing this one last glimpse of recognition from my ailing mother.

I go to my mother, kneel at her side. My niece, Nancy, is bent over her, giving her CPR, her recent stint in the Army having trained her for such emergencies. "Is she breathing?" I ask. She appears to be, but I grow frightened as I see my mother's eyes roll white into her head.

I think, *No. She can't die at my sister's wedding. It'd be too bitter, too cruel.* "Mamá, quédate con nosotros," I plead. "Te necesitamos, Mamá." And I watch as my voice summons her back. My brother comes and kneels at her other side.

"Mamá," I say. "Mira, aquí 'stá mi hermano, Mamá. Tu hijo."

She mumbles to him in Spanish.

"She shouldn't be drinking," my brother pronounces.

I turn to him. "That's not important now. Your mother is talking to you." I hold myself back from saying more.

"But I don't know what she's saying," he replies, meaning the Spanish.

"Just talk to her, James. She needs to hear your voice."

Within minutes the ambulance comes and drives my mother and me away in it, leaving the guests to somberly eat their wedding cake with the bride and groom. Soon after, my father and James meet me in the hospital waiting room, while my mother undergoes a series of brain scans and blood tests.

Sitting there, I find myself impatient with the perfunctory exchange of conversation among the three of us. This was not just a random accident. My mother was not well. She needed help. She needed home care and a proper distribution of medicine and companionship other than my father hiding out in his office. Some part of me remained incensed by the arrogance of my brother's counsel, which had led to the failed attempt at getting a home attendant for my mother.

Challenging my brother had always resulted in my humiliation . . . and failure. And my father never spoke up to my brother in his wife's defense. For decades, my sister and I had tried to intervene on our mother's behalf through letters, then emails, imploring our brother to visit her or at least to regularly call. Such efforts had only left my sister and me feeling ashamed, as if we had somehow misbehaved by confronting him.

"Protect your sisters" had been my mother's refrain to her son as JoAnn and I grew into womanhood. She didn't realize, however, that when she entreated James's brotherly protection she was speaking to the *American* side of the MexicanAmerican. James was trained to be a man of Mexican values in a gringo world where the values do not always translate. This was the missing piece to the cultural puzzle that my mother could never quite locate.

The only "protection" I remember from my brother was the heavy weight of his forearm over my shoulder when he required me to behave in a social situation. His arm held me in place.

He has me in a chokehold as I cross the threshold of his newlywed home.

"You feel okay?" His question directs the answer.

"Yeah." I pull away.

I hate him at that moment. Hate the disgrace of it. Hate that he felt he had to ask his wife's permission for me, the newly out lesbian, to be allowed in their home for a family dinner.

"I have to see how she feels about it," he had said to me during the one real conversation we ever had about my lesbianism.

It is 1977. We walk along the Berkeley Pier. The night bay waters surround us, an obsidian black.

"That's all right," I respond, really meaning to say, It's you I want, not her. But he had already betrayed me.

That day in the hospital waiting room, the best I can muster in my mother's defense is: "Now do you believe us?"

He glares back at me.

"This is not the time or place," my father quickly inserts for his own protection. He is nervous, complicit in the cover-up. I wonder when and where that time and place will ever occur.

In my brother's presence, I am no more than a girl.

The next morning, as JoAnn sets off for her honeymoon, my mother will enjoy a honeymoon of her own: a full weekend of hospital bed rest with my brother holding her hand at her bedside. Celia had been the one to make me ask him. "It's your sister's time to think of herself. And you have your own family to care for," she reminded me. (James had come to the wedding alone.) "Ask him to stay."

Remarkably, he agrees.

By late morning, my mother, sweetly drugged, falls into a dreamless sleep in her hospital bed, while my brother, father, and I meet for breakfast in a nearby Denny's. Seated at the table with the men of my family, my eyes measure my brother's and my indeterminate color against the mottled ivory of our father. Without my mother's presence, James and I blend generically white.

I would've liked to have told a "browner" history of my relationship with my brother where he hadn't believed he had to choose a life apart. From James's vantage point, as a well-heeled businessman with a family of Anglo-surnamed children, he may indeed have succeeded in erasing his Mexican past. For that's all, I feared, Mexicanism really meant to him: a past, embodied by the intractable will, old worldviews, and withering bones of his female elders. Simply put, there was no future in it.

From a Mexican point of view, however, family can never be disowned like property, cousins are not distant or once, twice, or three times removed. And "compadre" is as close to hermano as you can get.

December 1996.

Elvira spots her youngest brother, Eddie, in his usual rumpled khakis and smeared eyeglasses, slowly walking toward her down the blacktop driveway. The family has just learned of their brother Bobby's passing. My father stands at a distance and swallows the loss of his compadre, a thick lump in his throat. Elvira drops the garden hose, runs to meet Eddie, and falling into his arms, she just cries and cries and cries. I would've liked that in a brother.

Instead, James and I speak the language of logistics. Pickup and delivery schedules; my mother's projected discharge from the hospital. James confesses his concern, having witnessed his mother getting up from her hospital bed that morning and heading to the bathroom to "get ready for church."

"She thought she was home," he says, fearing her amnesia was the result of the head injury.

"She's been disoriented like that for some time now," I say. "It's normal," which portends something far worse.

The conversation falls silent.

In this town of fake lagoons and shopping malls, I glance across the Formica table at my closest living male relations. And there is no one there to assure me against the prospect of my oblivion: my life without a Mexican mother.

On Indigenous People's Day, my Mexican mother announced to my sister that the gringo who had occupied the other side of her bed for the last fifty-five years was not her husband. She refused to sleep with him again. She did not know who he was, she confessed, but she knew that she wasn't "his woman," and he had no business in her bed.

My sister is stunned. "Do you know who I am, Mom?"

"Yes," she said. "You're my daughter. I have three children."

"But Mom, that man is our father."

To which my mother replied, not hiding her disdain, "No. How could I have had children with that man?"

Joseph, my father, is a good man. He carries the privilege of goodness, if one can say that, in the sense that as a white man, although unassuming, he was often given the benefit of the doubt in his daily dealings with the outside world. Throughout most of my life, I observed how he was always presumed intelligent (which he is) and in charge (which was daily contradicted by my mother's stern rule at home). He was a man of few prejudices, a fact that I appreciated as I grew in awareness of social injustice and of my own sexual proclivities. Unlike my mother, he never had to discriminate, because he had never suffered overt discrimination. Yes, there was the horror of war, which he speaks of with a boy's tentative bravery and nostalgia. Something *was* lost there, or perhaps it was lost somewhere else; for in the world of confrontation, my father is a man riddled by fear.

His mother's life was one of serial "husbands," and Joseph's own childhood, one of serial "uncles"; familial language that taught him little about family. At the age of six, his father—a British Canadian—signed papers giving Joseph up for adoption to Hallie's third husband, an actor by the stage name of Dale _____.

This was the early-1930s period of "family" when Joseph, along with his little sister, Barbara, traveled up and down the southern coast of California, trailing behind their newly constituted parents. Dale and Hallie performed in tent shows pitched upon sandy and boardwalk beachfronts, the sound of breaking waves muffled behind a showman's megaphone announcements. A few years later, the actor would leave his "family" with nothing but his invented last name, which Joseph would carry for the rest of his life.

For most of my father's school years, through the late 1930s, Hallie raised her two children as a single mother, working with the WPA Federal Theater Project in San Francisco, my father's birthplace. While in high school, Joseph lied about his age and enlisted in the service. Soon after, World War II broke out and the United States Army would become "family," and for the first time in his life, Joseph had to clean and cook (KP duty) for himself and others. Then one day "family" disappeared in a sinking ship off the coast of the Philippines. Joseph was bunkered on the island within earshot of the bombing. Death so near, he imagined their cries as his own.

After six years of service, he returned home to the States to find "family" missing in action; his mother had remarried (this time to a "homosexual") and was soon divorced again, and Joseph could not resume the boyhood he had left in the scattered beach towns of Southern California. He was a young man now, free and white, with little more than the telegrapher skills he had learned in the service and a boy's bruised heart.

Joseph would endure a few lonely desert outpost jobs until he landed a spot working the graveyard shift at freight yards in Los Angeles. One Friday night, in the dancehall hours just before his midnight shift, Joseph buttoned up his out-of-style double-breasted suit and took a drive over to the Trianon Ballroom in South Gate. There, Joseph spotted "family" in the body of a five-foot-one, one-hundred-and-five-pound, drop-dead-gorgeous MexicanAmerican woman. She was older, he learned, and had been around the block of heartbreak more than a few times. She could certainly teach this young man a few things about "family," or so thought Joseph's mother. So, with Hallie's approval, and although "family" sent him away more than once, Joseph would not be dissuaded.

And with the ink still wet from Vera's divorce, Joseph married "family" and had children to make more "family" and when "family" almost died at forty-five when that one-hundred-and-five-pound "family" started shrinking away to eighty-five pounds in a Southern California hospital, well, Joseph saw quickly he was no "family" at all without Vera. No "family" at all for their three would-be orphaned children. And he drank hard for the first time in his life and got the car crashed and let the roaches wrestle with the Wheaties. And good thing for him and for those three would-be orphaned children that "family" gained weight and got well again. And "family" came home and warned, "I don't need you.

You'll be alone," if he didn't put that bottle down. So he put that bottle down finally, but couldn't figure out how to lift up "family" the way he knew she wanted.

Then suddenly, it is nearly fifty years later and "family" is back down to less than those eighty-five pounds and has forgotten how to cook and clean and keep "family" and can't even recognize the stranger across from her cup of coffee. So he-who-is-not-her-husband has to do a lot of growing up real fast and takes "family" to the restaurant two times a day, rolling in and out of the car on two useless hipbones, and even learns how to boil an egg and make oatmeal for her each morning. And he-who-is-not-her-husband does a little grocery shopping every few days right out of the drive-through dairy. He takes his own clothes to the laundry service and even picks up "family's" meds. These he gives to "family" two and three times a day, even when she refuses them, stubbornly turning her back to the expectant glass of water and the small pastel-colored hill of tablets. He very patiently waits, takes a breath, and pushes the pills toward her across the white broken-tiled kitchen bar, returning the small glass of water to the place in front of her. All the while, "family" berates him, batters him with her poison tongue. "I don't need you," she lies. And he remembers hearing the same refrain from her a half century before: *Men can come and go. All you've really got are your children.*

Eventually I would come to understand that the early abandonments my father suffered had made him very frightened in old age. If there is no family really, his actions told me, on whom can I rely? Nearly nine years younger than my mother, he was afraid the money would run out before he did. He made small compromises in my mother's care because care is expensive and time-consuming. He refused to recognize the days she went without bathing, the soiled clothes she wore day after day, the house smelling of his own denied incontinence because to acknowledge this would mean a change of life, a life they had constructed out of the fragile agreement of years of simply coping by looking away from each other and the disabling fact of old age.

My father had been born with a silver spoon in his mouth. How silver it was I didn't learn until his ninetieth birthday, when a Powerpoint display of his early life, gathered from recently uncovered family photographs, revealed a pre-Depression world of the latest-model automobiles and tastefully interiored homes.

In a studio portrait, the four-year-old sailor-suited Joseph Slatter plays poignantly with a toy sailboat. His dark-haired mother, Hallie, draped in the feathered fashion of the day, presses her cheek up against the lily head of her firstborn. Two years later, his father, the craftily entrepreneurial Burt Slatter, would float away from his family in an ocean of alcohol, not to return for decades. It was 1929, after all.

"This is an American story," Celia tells me. The boom and bust of wealth: the belonging and then the boot. But perhaps it is also an American story when a silver-spooned white boy ends up broke in Elvira's *Mexican*America. Not versed in Spanish, he would ironically survive all the Spanish-speakers of my mother's generation and emerge the repository of their stories, recalling dates and details long forgotten by Elvira and her siblings in the last years of their lives together.

In the years ahead, my father's skin would grow thinner and more translucent and he would easily return, culturally, to the

Anglo man he had always been. His marriage would become a memory propped up by the elegant aging face of Vera emblazoned upon a throw pillow. It would sit upon my father's assisted-living bed, placed there daily by the hand of a Spanish-speaking attendant.

It's the dementia talking," my father insisted.

True to her conviction, my mother moved out of the stranger-husband's bed and into the guest bed in the back of their small bungalow home.

And, of course, it was. But none of us could predict how long this delusion might last or if the next day Vera would wake up and suddenly recognize our father as her life companion. That day, she did not, and for many, many days and weeks to follow. This man was never her husband, she announced to everyone indignantly—her daughters, her last surviving sister, her doctor. She was done with the pretense.

Perhaps dementia really was the gift of old age, for JoAnn and I could not help but respond to the deeper messages relayed in Elvira's "locura." She was our mother, after all, flesh of our flesh, our soon-to-be ancestor, our tribal leader and once fierce matriarch, reduced to about six dozen pounds of bone-hard fury. As her Mexican female offspring, we saw in her the map of choices that had been drawn out for us, too. She was our mirror that day, the carnival fun-house kind—distorted and exaggerated, and funda-mentally marvelous. She offered hope for change: that the human spirit really wants truth; that the human spirit really wants free-dom; that the human spirit speaks even through a thick wall of dementia to remember the heart's history more profoundly than any chronology of facts about who married whom and who begot what children.

How my sister and I wanted to fight for our mother's right to this final freedom. Delusional or not, our freedom was also at stake here, our desperate need to believe that each of us has the capac-ity to change our lives, to choose a life not dictated by fear or, worse, habit. If you can't free yourself when you're looking at ninety, when can you?

Maybe our response to our mother's change of heart was a naïve refusal to accept the fundamental reality of her illness. We felt, regardless of her doctors' diagnoses, that her feelings de-served to be taken seriously. And then one morning you wake up to a phone call in which your mother announces that she no lon-ger recognizes her husband of fifty-plus years. *How could I have had children with that man!* And you don't know if it is a mo-ment of pure illumination, springing from the mind that resides wholly in the heart of a deeper knowing, or if the accumulated plaque in your mother's brain just closed off that synapse con-nected to the memory of her marriage.

We began to investigate alternative living arrangements that would allow our parents access to each other but would also pro-vide my mother the space from my father that she demanded. Since she could no longer take care of herself independently, we arranged for the two to live in separate quarters at the same assisted-living facility. He would be close by and she would be taken care of, the burden of which was debilitating to my father, to say nothing of how emotionally exhausted he had become from my mother's abuse. If getting away from "that man" was the pretext for allowing my mother a more tranquil heart, three healthy meals a day, and a monitored med intake (while supporting our father's right to remain her husband), we were going to move on it. My father agreed, though he was unsure about the move in general and, specifically, any move away from my mother.

My sister and I were not completely confident about this strategy. It was not the scenario we had anticipated in our younger years when it appeared our resilient mother would survive our father. The fact that our mother would become mentally disabled while our father remained of sound mind forced JoAnn and me to quickly rewrite what would become the last pages of our mother's life.

It had been several weeks since my mother had declared her independence from my father and moved to the back bedroom. My sister had managed to get a woman, una mexicana, to spend several hours, three or so days a week, assisting my mother around the house. This woman was an irritation to my mother, that much was clear, but she was permitted entrance into the inner sanctum of Elvira's home under the pretext that it was for my father, who had finally agreed to hip surgery.

The attendant had been with my parents no more than a week when I received a call from my father. "She's saying words to me that I never before heard come out of her mouth. S-h-i-t," he spells it. "And "h-o-r-e," he spells it wrongly, and I remember what a polite man my father is. The attendant tells him that she's seen worse, both husband and wife terribly cruel to each other. "You are kind to her," she tells my father. My mom gets on the phone, irate. She accuses my father of having an affair with the home attendant, which I knew was not so. Her language cruder than I ever remember, I can barely stand her vulgarity, even under these circumstances.

I plead with her, "Mom, you never used to talk to me this way."

She doesn't give a damn, she says, and I know it is her illness, but there is something else at work here. I hold fast to my belief that this is just another way of my mother saying she wants out. I cannot ignore the fact, nor can I stay on the phone and endure the obscenities rushing from her mouth. I find an excuse to cut the connection against her rising fury.

Twenty minutes later when I call back, my father picks up. He reminds me once again of the dates for his hip surgery. Since the day he agreed to the operation, his health has been the singular subject on his mind. "Put Mom on the phone," I say. As he hands it to her, I hear her, suddenly meek, asking her husband, "Do you want me to be there in the hospital with you?" Vera is now holding on to the last semblance of what it means to be a wife. *Does he still need her?* she is asking.

"Of course," he answers.

I promise to personally pick her up and stay with her and take her to and from the hospital as much as she wants. But I can't shake the profanities from a half hour before. I can no longer count on the mother I know being on the other end of the telephone line when I pick up the receiver.

I couldn't save her, I was quickly beginning to realize. And maybe there was relief in this, a small, pitiful, selfish relief that I did not have to drop my life to pick up hers. Yet there were times when I knew that the only thing that would satisfy my own anxious heart was to gather her up and bring her home to me. It remained my final exit plan for my mom, if lodged nowhere but in the back of my own forgetful mind. I had always imagined that my loyalty to my mother was such that I would do anything to make her life bearable in her old age. But nothing would make it bearable, I was beginning to realize—assisted living, living with me, anything involving living. Meanwhile, JoAnn and I continued to try to negotiate a settlement of place *and heart* for our mother.

We had already been stung by our first attempt, sixteen months earlier, to get our mother a daily attendant, and over the course of those sixteen months we had learned the hard way the difference between Elvira's theoretical agreement to something and its practical implications. In this case, we knew our mother's agreement to consider assisted living, which had surfaced in several conversations with her, fell squarely into the category of theory.

After JoAnn and I visited a number of facilities within a few miles' radius of my sister's new home in Orange County, and landed on one that was to my father's liking, my sister and I moved in for the attack. This was no chess game, but a battle of courage in the face of my mother's desperate fear. We had to convince her that we were on her side when everything about our actions told her we were the enemy.

On that Halloween morning, my mother had awakened remembering neither our discussion about assisted living nor her recent "divorce" from my father. As such, it was relatively easy to get her and my father up and out of the house to meet my sister at Prestige. We noticed that many of the newest facilities carried names marketed to intentionally contradict the reality of elders' increasing dependence as they aged. "Sunrise" perversely offered elders a place to live in the quickening sunset of their years.

But that day I am grateful for the lie in the euphemism (which I guess is the point), as I am for the resort-hotel style of the building, with its fireplaced lobby and elegant dining room of pastel tablecloths and upholstered chairs. My mom likes the joint, which briefly relieves us, her traitor-daughters, who usher her in for a complimentary breakfast. She innocently eats her basted eggs and perfectly crisped bacon as her family moves in for the kill.

My mother is in rare form, charming the staff with niceties; but we know she isn't getting what's going on. As far as she can see, we are . . . window-shopping. "This is very nice," she says. "Someday when I'm older . . ." and I don't even bother to hear the rest. This day was less than one week before her eighty-ninth birthday. For an instant, my sister and I catch each other's glance. Our eyes shift back to our plates as we each strategize the next move. Suddenly, the goodwill emissary salvadoreña server does the job for us. "It's a great place to live," she says. "You will be very happy here."

That was it. The meal was over. Bolting upright in her chair, Elvira tosses down her fork. She can barely stay in her seat, she is so incensed, scooping the napkin up into a ball in her lap, her eyes darting around the room for an exit.

"Mom, you can't take care of yourself anymore," I say. The server, realizing what she has done, slinks away.

"Fine, throw me in the trash can, if that's all I'm good for." She was right. No amount of finery was going to make this place anything other than a trash can to my mom. Plain and simple, it was not her home.

"I don't care what you damn kids do to me," she continues, her anger spilling out into the lobby. She spies my dad. "And look at him. You think he loves me?"

"I do, honey . . ." he mutters weakly.

"I don't want your lies no more. I'm getting out of here!"

But this time we will not relent; it took too much effort to get her here. We will not let her leave without at least speaking with the director. "He just has some questions for you," I plead. "You can go home after that, Mom."

Everything depends on my mother behaving well in the interview. The more independent she is, the less the cost; the more independent she is, the less traumatic the transition, we hope. Afraid of a scene, we walk her out to the patio, where the director greets us. He goes into his sales pitch, which really is of no importance to my mother, who is fixed on one thought: getting the hell out of there. As he urges my mother to "merely answer a few questions," a parade of demented elders pass behind my mother's back and across the patio. I quickly recognize them as being from the memory unit, Expressions. This is the dementia-care program we are trying desperately to *avoid*, if only Elvira would cooperate. The residents march past happily enough, their faces made-up like cartoon animals, sporting pointed ears and painted-on whiskers.

At first, I am confused by their outfits, and then remember it is Halloween. Holding hands, they move along with that telltale small-stepped shuffle that I would later recognize in my own mother. I instinctually move behind her to block her from turning in the parade's direction. Still, some part of me can't help but laugh inside at the absurdity of the moment. I recall the late-sixties French film *The King of Hearts*, in which Alan Bates, during World War I, happens upon a French town that has been abandoned to the suddenly liberated inmates of an insane asylum. *Who really are the crazy ones here?* the film asks, as do I. Certainly not my mother, who fights to keep the last vestiges of her identity intact.

My mother begs the kind director's understanding. He does not know the full extent of the abuse she endures, the insufferable laziness of my father, the neglect from my sister. I try to intervene, fearing the more my mother talks, the closer she is to failing her "entrance exam" to Prestige. She turns on my sister, assuming (correctly) that she is the principal conspirator behind this latest movida to render her life worthless.

"And you, what about your own daughters?" she says to JoAnn with complete disdain. "They're good for nothing." Her tone is suggestive, lewd. My sister is speechless. My mother adores JoAnn's daughters, especially her firstborn, Erin, who as the eldest spent the most time with her grandmother, making mud pies in the backyard, sharing teatime and talking about their "no-good husbands." Erin es la consentida entre los nietos, y la Rebecca su "baby." Pero ni modo, because this is an old tune for my mother. When she had no other way to stop us, she tried to stop us with our sex.

I would have to become a mother myself to finally comprehend that my mother's vulgar rampages against us as young women were prompted by her raw fear of losing control of us and of her own life. That day on the patio of Prestige Assisted Living, more than thirty years later, there was no mistaking it for anything else.

"That's enough, Mom," I say to cut her off from her crude tirade against JoAnn and her daughters.

She storms out the patio, through the lobby, and out the front doors of the building. As in her meetings with the psychiatrist, she does not wander. How could she? *Wander* means to move about aimlessly. There is nothing aimless in my mother's being. She stands riveted to the railing outside the front door of the building; she is fixed in her intention to resist.

"I'll go talk to her," I say to JoAnn.

I go outside. I make her sit down with me. She grips the arms of the wrought-iron chair, her knuckles white with fear. I give it all that I've got.

"Do you believe that I love you?" I must convince her that I am the exception, that she can trust me; that I alone will make sure she is not harmed. "Do you trust me?" I ask. And she has to say yes, because without me, at that moment, she has nothing and nowhere to go beyond that railing. She knows where home is, and right now it resides inside whatever shred of confidence she has left in her youngest daughter.

"Just answer the man's questions, Mom. That's all I ask, please. Just do this for me." And she does. For me, her youngest. "The only one who really knows how to love."

Putting her "strangers' face" back on, my mother passes her interview with flying colors. Both my father and my mother would be able to come and go from their apartment as they pleased, while having their laundry and housekeeping done by the staff, meds administered and monitored by professionals, and meals provided in the main dining room. Prestige is only two miles from my sister's new home, and we would no longer have to worry about Elvira burning the house down or finding her laid up on the couch in a drug-induced stupor. The house would be put on the market at a price good enough to secure a two-bedroom apartment at Prestige. At least for the time being, my mother would have her own room and bed and this might just ward off any further anxieties she holds about my father's encroachment.

All this, our most "prestigious" and never-to-be-realized dream plan.

A MOTHER'S DICTUM

*V*era . . ."

She is backed up against the kitchen sink, holding a steak knife in front of her. "Don't touch me," she warns. "I'll kill you."

"Honey, don't," Joseph implores, but he is not her husband, not in Vera's mind.

He doesn't know how they got to this place, this nightmare of their whole life together denied or obliterated or unremembered. He doesn't know which.

His wife had been asleep for hours. Turning off the evening news, Joseph rises from the couch with difficulty. He drags his slippered feet across the hardwood hallway floor toward their bedroom. Tonight, he is encouraged to see that his wife has gone to sleep in their shared bed. Maybe in the morning she will be better, he thinks. Maybe Vera will have forgotten her weeks-long standoff against him. He had not protested her departure from their bed. He missed her, but knew there was no point in protesting.

He silently removes his bathrobe and maneuvers his way under the covers on his side of the bed. It is difficult to get in without disturbing her. His shattered hips refusing to comply, he cannot really slide nor lift them completely. Still, he manages to find a spot where both hips settle themselves more or less comfortably. He contemplates the steady sound of his wife's breathing.

As she sleeps, he can imagine Vera returned to him, nagging and easily irritated, but also lighthearted and full of so much to say about people, the small injustices of life; she, always the protagonist of the highest standards. He used to enjoy their conversations, coming in for lunch from the garage-office at noontime to catch *The Young and the Restless* over a tuna sandwich and a cup of coffee. He had never thought he could like soap operas, but once they hooked him, that was it. It was something they shared. He remembers this, as her light snoring sends him off to sleep.

"Get the hell out of my bed!" He is suddenly awakened to the bright light overhead and his wife's constricted face hovering above him. "What are you doing in my bed? Get out! Get out!"

She pummels his face and chest with her fists. He tries to grab her flailing arms, but she is too quick for him. She runs into the kitchen. He hears a drawer open and slam shut. He struggles to get out of the bed, but the stiffness in his hips paralyzes him. He finally hurls himself up and at the door, stumbling into the kitchen.

He goes to her, easily overpowers her, separating her grip from the knife. She, equally easily, slips away from him because he has never held her against her will. "If you ever hit me, I'll leave you." He remembers her refrain from their early years. "I'll take the kids." Elvira rushes out the back door and flies up the steps to the backyard apartment, her adrenaline giving her wings. She pounds on the door of the neighbor, a MexicanAmerican woman in her thirties, a "nice girl" whom Elvira has come to trust and who, by sheer physical proximity, has been witness to many of her rampages against her husband.

"He's trying to kill me," she cries.

Joseph hears this and does not follow her; the steps up to the second-story apartment are too much for him. He waits for the neighbor to come down to talk.

"I didn't touch her," he says when she meets him at the bottom of the stairs; and then adds, "I think we should call my daughter."

They telephone my sister, the lionhearted one. She reminds our father that the doctor had prescribed a tranquilizer in case of an emergency. Could he find it in the cupboard? With the neighbor holding the phone, he locates the drug on a high shelf in the kitchen. Hanging up, the good neighbor talks my mother into taking the pill, and moments later, Elvira is calm enough to return to the guest bed in the back of the house. But Joseph cannot sleep knowing that he cannot live like this anymore; that even losing the house, his small tax business, his life as he knows it, would be preferable to this, the worst day of his life.

JoAnn called it "the worst day of my life," the day she had to *institutionalize* our mother. A harsh word, but one that accurately describes our decision to relinquish our mother into a system of strangers, who could never know the nuances of her pain regardless of its cause—amyloidal plaque in the brain o una vida de puro resentimiento.

That morning, my mother had awakened from her tranquilizer-induced sleep, disoriented but rested. Per the doctor's instructions, my sister came to pick her up to admit her into Huntington Hospital in Pasadena, for psychiatric anxiety and paranoia. My father complied with the plan, staying out of our mother's way and remaining in the hospital waiting room for long hours, both relieved to not have to witness his wife's incarceration, for he knew it would be against her will, and also disturbed that it had come to this.

The fact that our father, our mother's daily companion, would serve as the object of her deepest fear and derision continued to rack our minds and hearts. To her daughters, our mother's response was at once perfectly logical, the culmination of a half century of complaint; and, at the same time, witnessing our father's sorrow, it seemed horribly cruel and unthinkable. But the reality was that our mother was suffering without reprieve. Her rages would end up killing her or someone else. Her pitiful assault against my father had forced us to act.

For the first hour or so, admission to Huntington Hospital went peaceably enough. My mom was sequestered in a private room where my sister continued to try to entertain her, assuring her all would be okay. But as time passed without word from hospital staff (they were trying to find a vacant bed for my mom in the psychiatric wing), my mother's anxiety mushroomed. Over the course of many hours, my sister left the room several times in an attempt to communicate with a hospital staff that remained unresponsive.

One time, the last time, she had stayed away too long. By the time JoAnn returned, my mother had torn up the room that had been locked from the outside, raging that she had been abandoned by everyone, *even her own ingrata daughter, who had just dumped her like a sack of potatoes. If she could only find her pocketbook, she'd call a taxi right now. Where did they put her money? They stole it. She knew they stole it. When she got outta there, she was gointu get her own place. She was tired of it all. She didn't give a damn no more what people thought of her. She was getting out.*

I didn't see my mother's face when JoAnn stepped back into

that room, but I can picture it. Since childhood, I had seen that look of utter contempt thrown at my father and sister so many times, many more times than it was hurled at my brother or me. It is a look that freezes the heart; and when it comes at you, your heart scrambles for the warmth of one good thought to keep the organ pumping, loving. Because to be on the receiving end of that look, where in my mother's eyes you are beyond redemption, you think you may never love again.

I don't know why my mother was so hard on my dad and sister, maybe because she could be, maybe because they didn't fight back. At least, that was the case with my father, and I suspect it is one of the reasons Elvira resented him so.

I remember after my mother became ill, Auntie Eva confided in me that my mother had been hit only once in marriage. "She had slapped him first," referring to my mother's first husband. "She had it coming to her." I didn't know if this was my auntie's version of the story or my mother's, who always said she'd leave any marriage if a man laid a hand on her. And, apparently, the fight was precisely about that, about leaving him. The fact that the man must have outweighed my mother by nearly a hundred pounds made it sound like an unfair match to me.

But I believed it, believed there was a longing in my mother to be put solidly *in place*, to be relieved of herself, of being so damn in charge, so right about so much and yes, that first husband had been a womanizer, a military man with a woman for every furlough, and yes, she would have to leave him. But it seems he desired her, and that was *something*. To be taken in that way, not by a man who was good for you, not by a man who would give you children and stick around to support those children, but just by someone who unequivocally wanted you and was not afraid to show it.

Thinking of Elvira's romances as a young woman, Celia goads

me, "C'mon, Cherríe, you don't really believe your mom was a virgin until she was married in her late twenties, do you?"

Yes, I answer. Because she said so.

Because it mattered so much to her—to hold the example for her younger siblings, while neither her mother (after her husband's death and still in her forties) nor her divorced sisters felt similarly obliged. Perhaps my mother's virginity until marriage was a technicality; perhaps abstinence was simply required to ward off an unwanted pregnancy in a woman who was the primary support of her familia. One thing is for sure, her virginity was not for lack of passion.

Speaking of my parents' troubled years in the early 1960s, my mother once admitted, "I shouldn't have turned away from your father for so long. One time, I put my feet close to him in the bed, just to touch him, and he pulled away from me. And that was it." But *was* that it? Surely it was not her last gesture to connect. But who was this woman, beneath all the raging, that was so vulnerable to a man's rejection?

In his wish to write a story of desire between my parents, my brother once recounted how, as a grown man, he had, without calling first, dropped in on them unexpectedly, only to find them nervously coming out of the back room. They were "undone" in a way that suggested sex. I don't doubt the sex, at least in the early years. I regularly remember the fresh smell of vinegar in the bathroom on early mornings and encountering my mother's "women supplies" in the bottom drawer that held the vinegar bottle, the red rubber douche bag, the white snakelike tubing: the ritual elements of my mother's postcoital hygiene.

I like the story of it as well; to picture our parents beyond middle age, generating some fire in their relationship. But perhaps it wasn't exactly fire that endured between them, as much as warmth, a spontaneous warmth I witnessed in those years—before the loss of cognition and ruined hips—when money was plentiful enough and Grama Dolores, along with the world of worry she had brought into their lives, had passed on.

On a balmy summer night, my parents stare out onto the Caribbean waters and contemplate the moon's reflection from a cruise ship deck. They are alone at that midnight hour, standing side by side, warmed by nostalgia and a few after-dinner cocktails. They had taken to the dance floor earlier in the evening, Vera limber and straight-backed in the knowing arms of her husband. They glide and spin about the dance floor to a big-band sound in full throttle, a could-be Ella Fitzgerald extemporizing to "How High the Moon."

Peering into the moonlit sea, Vera says to her husband, "I never thought I'd ever get to see something so beautiful like this."

She remembers a long-ago fortune-teller prophesying, "You will travel all over the world."

There was a kind of romance in this moment for both my parents. He saw it as shared with her. She felt it as a singular part of her own private destiny.

I often wondered why my mother ended up marrying white. Elvira had had other loves before the two gringo marriages. Mexican men—mujeriegos and sweet-talkers—who possessed the beauty, charm, intelligence, and deceit of her father and eldest brother. Perhaps she just ran out of time or hope; for some part of her would always experience Anglos as "others"; not foreign exactly, but just a cavernous hyphen between cultures.

With wild animal eyes, Elvira searches the hospital room for an exit. She sees my sister, standing frozen before her, yet another jailer in the way of her escape. She grabs JoAnn's purse, begins to frantically rummage through it.

"What is it, Mom? What do you want?"

She pulls out her address book, and trying to regain her calm, begins to methodically count out the letters. She reads, "M . . . O . . . N . . . T . . . E . . . B . . ." Flipping pages, she goes on, reading the letters of names and addresses: "G . . . A . . . R . . . C . . . I . . . A." They do not form words. Another page: "C . . . H . . . A . . ."

"I shoulda taught myself," she cries. "I shoulda made myself learn."

This prison is her fault, she thinks. Had she educated herself, she wouldn't be in this situation, powerless among the gringos. She couldn't even last a few weeks in adult school. Pendeja. That was what was wrong with her brain: not her memory, but education. Had she gone back to school, she coulda written her way out of this prison.

Or so she desperately needed to believe. Elvira was no victim.

JoAnn was shocked to see that our mother could no longer recognize the written names of people and places she had known for decades. Yes, Elvira had little formal education, but she could at least read and write that much; as she could read the recipes of the *Betty Crocker Cookbook* when she needed to and, after a lifetime of pieced-together learning, even the front page of the *L.A. Times*.

Nearing fifty, my mother used to sit in the kitchen and hold the newspaper away from her at a full arm's length, straining to decipher the letters through failing eyesight. Resolute, Elvira silently mouthed the words as she read; in the same way she picked out the Hallmark cards from the hundreds displayed at the nearby Save-On; in the same way she signed birthday and Christmas cards in a strained cursive for her children and grandchildren.

I recall that during our elementary school years, our mother once actually acted upon her constant lament that she had been denied an education. We were living in San Gabriel by then, and since her three children were grown enough to be home alone at night, Elvira slipped out to take English reading and writing classes at the local public high school. I remember her, in the late evenings, laboring over her composition workbook and my feeling a kind of curious superiority. The tasks inside seemed so simple to me. But we never lorded this over our mother. We very much wanted her to learn.

The trouble was that my mother's spoken English was perfect, as was her Spanish. She was fluidly bilingual in conversation and functionally illiterate on the page in both languages. Unlike her youngest brother and sister, who had garnered some Mexican schooling as children, followed by high school in the United States (which my breadwinner mother had insisted upon against the wishes of their mother), the specific conditions of Elvira's binational gap in literacy seemed impossible to overcome. Plus, it was too damn humiliating.

So, after a few weeks of having served as translator, community liaison, and social worker for her monolingual mexicano classmates (exchanging leads for jobs, childcare, y una buena sobadora), Elvira closed the book on her formal education and continued to use the fluency she knew best. She could walk and talk us out of most crises; and she deferred to her well-schooled children and her husband to maneuver the world of letters—check writing, job applications, and school permission forms. But that day in the psychiatric hospital, the world of letters came crashing down upon Elvira, without husband or child, as she saw it, to help dig her way out of the wreckage.

I have no real idea what my mother thought on this, the first day of many incarcerations to come. I have only my sister's story of unbearable sadness as she accompanied my mother, who was transported by wheelchair from the main hospital to the Della Martin Center psychiatric wing. I would fly down from Oakland in the next few days.

"This is the most direct route," the hospital aide assures my sister. They travel through a maze of underground passageways beneath the hospital. Low-hanging air-conditioning ducts and water pipes cast moving shadows across their faces. Elvira thrashes in the chair, banging her feet and dragging her heels against the unyielding cement floor. She is determined to stop this diabla steering her to hell.

It was a horror film that JoAnn alone experienced, one that drew from the worst of our girlhood repertoire of grainy gray psycho films. And she, faithless daughter, was submitting our mother to this heartless drama. For I know this is how my sister felt. I know that in order to get my mother help, JoAnn had to counter every bit of self-doubt she carried and act above and beyond my mother's violent protests. She had to be bigger than my mother. And this tore at the most elemental fabric of their fifty-two-year relationship.

My sister had never talked back to our mother, not since her early teen years of Hollywood dreams and romantic dark-skinned beaus. My sister's boldest acts of rebellion, or better said, resistance, ended by age eleven or twelve, just as puberty fell like an anvil of hopelessness upon our gender-restricted lives. Before that, before breasts and periods and pimples and maternal admonitions in the name of virginity, my sister wanted great things—movie stardom, international travel, and the free mind of books—and she had stood up for her cause with a tearless opposition against my mother's lashing tongue and leather belt.

"Cry, JoAnn," I begged. It was all that our mother required. She'd stop hitting when the tears started flowing. But JoAnn would never cry, no matter how much I begged, the sting of the lash fresh on my own summer-naked legs. JoAnn would not submit and could not escape as my brother had. The moment he'd hear the metal belt buckle lifting off its nail hook behind the service porch door, he was out that door, my mother whipping the wind behind him.

Ironically, JoAnn was the daughter who stopped rebelling, ending up closest to home, and made four grandchildren, to her mother's delight and perennial worry. In that sense, maybe she had been the most faithful to my mother, she who always doubted my mother's faithfulness to her.

I remember so many of my mother's dictums from when I was growing up—*dichos*, as they are called in Spanish—sayings by which we construct a life. "I may forgive, but I never forget" was one of Elvira's most salient and was usually invoked after a particularly grievous act of disloyalty enacted by some relation. Locking her mother up that night, my sister knew the reverse had finally become true. Elvira would surely *forget* what had finally closed the keyless door on everything she understood as a life. But, my god, could whatever remained of our mother ever *forgive* us this beleaguered act of love?

PART III

ELVIRA'S COUNTRY

The spiritual country of the human is a sensed world, not
a known one. It's a world where, put into words, meaning vanishes.

—LINDA HOGAN

From as early as I can remember, I thought of God and my
mother as a kind of symbiotic unit. Hers was a faith no
church could contain, since no church could contain my
mother. She was a rebel in this regard, who turned to her home
altar more confidently than any communion rail, who calculated
the Catholic Church's rules to her benefit, refusing to marry my
father in the Church until she could wager, after her eldest child's
twelfth birthday, that the marriage might last. Until then, she had
been technically "living in sin," as her children's Catholic school
teachers instructed. And in that resided my first critical stance in
relation to the Catholic Church. If the Church said my mother
was a sinner, there was something wrong with the Church.

My mother was a renegade of a Spanish-turned-gringo Catholicism that could never respond to the full depth of her faith. Even
after the small wedding at La Placita Church in Los Angeles, and,
as an elder, in tandem with my father, receiving her Confirmation, my mother's spirit life had prevailed over the encumbrances

of clergy and ecclesiastic law. I knew, as she knelt beside me at Sunday Mass, as I would one day witness at her own funeral, these rites did not house her ways of knowing.

Once my mother was admitted to the psychiatric wing, under thirty-day observation, and officially diagnosed with advanced Alzheimer's, we knew she would not be returning home. As coincidence or fate would have it, my father would several days later be admitted into a nearby hospital for hip surgery; and I would sleep alone in my childhood home for the first time in my life.

During the first few nights of my stay, I was awakened by a spirit presence, a palpable sensation of disquiet inside the walls of the house, especially in the back room where my mother's altar stood abandoned, small plastic children's toys and the smoked glass of an empty veladora awaiting her return. This is where my mother had spent her last nights of tormented sleep.

There was nothing malevolent in the ánimo spinning down the hallway and in and out of rooms; only that the house felt alive with the memories Elvira had finally left forgotten inside those walls. Suddenly, to occupy that house without the physical presence of my mother was to stand inside the depth and breadth of the spirit life her small frame had carried for nearly a century. Without her physically there, her ghosts had been let loose to wander the rooms of that two-bedroom 1920s stucco house in search of her. There was no question in my mind that it was she they sought, she who in her last years at home straddled that seamless divide between visible and incarnate life.

During those years, I had watched my mother begin to cultivate her dead ancestor relatives as her daily intimates. Spirit relations had come to reside in that small white house and increased in meaning as my mother's remembered world lessened in importance. It was as if in a lapsed moment of synapse connection they had snuck in to inhabit my mother's psyche. That's one way to think of it. The Chickasaw writer Linda Hogan describes her own experience with amnesia as "a country of ghosts, a no-woman's land [where] the daily details of a life no longer count." This "country of ghosts" was the world my mother came to prefer over the intrusions of caretakers trying in vain to tether her to our more mundane world.

Elvira, she who had *la facultad*, as Gloria Anzaldúa called it, to carry all those ghost stories inside of her. How was I to honor them and their carrier in a twenty-first-century AngloAmerica where to reside with the spirits is to reside in a foreign country? We were so far from home, it felt to me—my mother and me—living out her final years in this nation of true amnesiacs that could not contain her calling.

But that small white house, a house for which I believed I held no nostalgia, a house I had to leave in order to live, a house I marked as the site and source of my rebellion, had been *country* to my mother. It had allowed her permission to know what she knew and to reign madre over all of it, even as it occulted itself within the parameters of that narrow lot of crabgrass and rose garden in the smoggy basin of Los Angeles County.

Are these small plots of lot and land what is left of memory as Mexicans in the United States?

Is this how ancestral memory returns to us, indifferent to the generation and geography of borders?

That night, alone in my mother's house, for it was hers, not my father's, as those abandoned espíritus made clear to me, I swallowed our Mexican Indian herencia in hard gulps of conciencia. It was she they missed, she who heard and spoke to them, she who had made daily offerings to them through finger-worn novena booklets, smoking veladoras, and a few folded dollar bills slipped beneath the altar cloth.

But I had to get some sleep.

I remember my Celia's consejo: if you want spirits to go away you have to tell them so. I get out of bed and implore my mother's spirit keepers. "She's not here," I say aloud, my voice dropping to a register of authority. "Now let me sleep."

And, miraculously, they do.

Before succumbing to sleep, however, I make a promise to them; I will come back and put this house to rest. In my next visit, I will bring medicine to help us all—spirits and the living—make this crossing.

SWEET LOCURA

hen I first spy my mother in the psychiatric wing, she *is* my mother and that is all that matters to me; that she is recognizable and that she looks back at me with that same light of recognition. I had learned from my sister that those first few days before my arrival had been the hardest. Each day JoAnn would find our mother latched inside a kind of adult-sized high chair that could be released only by the attendant.

As JoAnn approached, my mother would scarcely acknowledge her. Hunched over the tray of the high chair, my mother applied her full concentration to folding a paper napkin into smaller and smaller fractions. When her folding could go no further, she'd open up the napkin and begin again, her arthritic fingers pleating and pressing the thinning paper over and over. Elvira must have derived a kind of comfort from the fine movement of her fingers, for it was an activity she would return to often over the next few years, especially when there was little impulse to respond to those around her.

On the day that I arrive, however, she is remarkably "present."

"Mamá," I call to her, feigning a casualness I could not possibly possess in that moment. She sits in the high chair, situated in the corner of a narrow dining-rec room of molded plastic chairs and long mess-hall-style tables. A large TV chatters in the corner. A few patients are gathered around it, others milling in and out of the room, others laid out in full stupors in La-Z-Boy recliners. Upon the sight of me, my mother immediately brightens. She opens her arms to me, *"Ay, mi'ja!"* She is elated to see me, no trace of rancor in her face. For the next twenty months, my mother, most times, could be counted on to greet me in just that way. "Mi'ja," my daughter. "Mi'jita," my little daughter.

The translation cannot possibly express the pure grounding provided by that word for a Mexican child of any age. In a gesture of familial confidence, parents and tíos and abuelitas and even strangers tell it to us. So that, in a certain way, entre nosotros mexicanos here in an English-speaking world, it denotes the extended Familia de la Raza. A child knows instinctively whom to trust (or not) when that word is relayed between generations. For this reason, I have never called a lover "mi'ja," nor allowed my peers to do so with me. It was a word reserved for my elders. It was the one thing that made the slow pain of losing my mother bearable; for when she could not remember my name, she always remembered "mi'ja."

After a day's visit, of JoAnn and me escorting our mother in and out of the dining and activity rooms, Elvira asks me to go to the bathroom with her. There she borrows my comb to arrange her hair, wild from waning permanented curl and dark chestnut dye. She then accompanies us to the double remote-controlled doors to say goodbye. My sister and I are both nervous, fearful that with her newfound lucidity, she will want to come with us, fearful that we will have to reenact the trauma of relinquishing her to this place all over again. I hold my mother's forearm against her unsteady gait as we make our way down the corridor. Her arm is pure vein and muscle, a road map of scars decades old, etched into the graying parchment of her skin. My mother and I share this: the hands and arms of worker women—stove burns and the abraded skin of decades of bleach and household detergent; the calluses of yard work, rose thorns, and heavy lifting.

We make idle conversation as we near the door. I spy the attendant and with my eyes ask her to back us up as my sister and I take our leave. My mother and I embrace as I tell her that she has to stay. "You can't leave now, Mom. Los doctores . . ." and then I mumble something by way of explanation. She is, for a moment, disoriented. Then she quietly complies. I observe her childlike wonder as we turn to leave and the door closes heavily before her. But in that final second, I glimpse her moving toward the attendant, having already forgotten we were there.

On the other side of the door, my sister and I giggle nervously at the sheer marvel of our mother's release of us. It is the first time in forever that my sister can remember our mother not being angry with her for *something*. The miracle of drugs, we think. For the first time we are hopeful that our mother might not go unto death in a fit of rage. For the first time, we imagine the possibility of peace for her and *awareness*, a slow, gentle letting go of all attachment, including her children. For the first time, the illness holds the fragile promise of benevolence.

Driving along Foothill Boulevard, I take the long way back to my parents' house. The San Gabriel Mountains bear witness. Languorous gray silhouetted beasts, they remain my companions after so many years away from this valley. I loved watching those mountains as a child, bemoaned their disappearance in the summertime, when the smog fell like an iron curtain between hope and us. This was how it felt in those days, as if the smog had penned us in somehow, so close and yet so far from the muffled voices of Black and Brown rebellion in that late-1960s inner city just down the road from us. But when those Santa Ana winds kicked up and cleansed the Valley with their sweet loca currents, the mountains would reveal themselves personally to me. They were my emblems of hope; they compelled me to believe there was freedom on the other side.

SEND THEM FLYING HOME

I used to think the house mattered. Just a few months earlier, I had advocated for the importance of my mother's daily rituals as a way to keep her grounded in her world: each morning taking a bowl of milk out to the street cat she had adopted; washing a few items of clothing; making the bed as expertly as she did when I was a young girl. Later I was not convinced that anything mattered to my mother except the events that transpired in the prison that was her scarred brain.

In retrospect, I was weak. My sister's hurry to clear out the house became my own excuse to avoid not only disagreement with JoAnn, but something else, something I could not quite say at the time. I only knew I held inside me a reserve—a holdout for Elvira that wanted to listen to each and every ghost she had abandoned inside those walls; that I wanted to take months to do so; that I felt they and she deserved at least that much. Maybe it is called spirit work. Maybe it is simply a matter of knowing that objects hold meaning. But in my weakness, I settled for three solitary days instead of three months.

To say that closing up my mother's house conjured strong memories would be to pretend to a kind of openheartedness I did not possess at the time. I found myself going through the motions, as it were, because the family body—living and ancestral—needed so much more time than this to inhabit the loss. In self-defense, I told myself that I already knew my mother's secrets. What I didn't know was the mystery behind my own impassiveness. Where *was* my heart?

Where was that daughter who had been the privileged ear of her mother's confianza? La niña who believed nobody was ever good enough for Elvira? No one could match her mother's beauty and integrity, an innate intelligence that far outweighed the educated "foreigners"—the American nuns and laypersons—who stood before la niña in institutional-green classrooms, pressed beneath mission tiles and Anglo appropriation.

I would never have thought to use such words then, for it was a wordless knowing—this half-century battle I was to fight against my family's inevitable conversion to suburban stupor.

In many ways, moving through that house was to move through the clutter of my mother's mind. It was as if the house were a kind of three-dimensional staging of her life story—from health to illness, from order to what seemed like pure chaos, but at a deeper level that reflected its own strange ecosystem. Each cupboard and every drawer contained what appeared to be representative objects from every aspect of my mother's daily domestic life: bras with their small foam cups stuffed into the same drawer with hair rollers, unpaid bills, loose change, a used dye bottle, a small box of costume jewelry, family snapshots inside unsealed envelopes, a half-used tube of Bengay, an old brown sock, prescription bottles, and holy cards, so many holy cards.

Buried in the corners of closets was more of the same: a stuffed animal from my son's toddler days, a clean wrinkled pair of my dad's boxers, a drugstore bag of unopened cosmetics. There had been so many missing items and occasionally, yes, that "stolen" identification card, set of house keys, checkbook, and new scarf would emerge, but even after my many days alone in the house and later after my sister's arrival with her adult children, our excavation produced few great revelations as to the mysteries of those years of loss. Maybe the jardineros really *had* come in and taken her watch. We'd never know. So much of my mother's life had fallen into a great Diablo Triangle of unsolved missing parts, as if the physical objects of my mother's history had simply vanished with her own vanishing memory.

At the same time, whole drawers of perfectly starched manteles remained expertly folded, alongside pastel table napkins and hand-embroidered doilies that hadn't been touched in decades. To open this world of order, where telas were starched and guardadas for that special visita, one felt drawn into a forgotten era; where after daylong mornings of labor en la casa o en el campo, señoritas were confined to embroidery hoops to pass those endless hot afternoons, under the watchful eye de la tía o de la hermana mayor.

My mother had tried in vain to instruct my sister and me in the tradition. "It's for your hope chest," she encouraged. To my bookish sister, who fantasized a romantic rescue from the humdrum of her Catholic school girlhood, a hope chest conjured the figure of a brooding dark and handsome figure on the horizon, one akin to those from the nineteenth-century novels of which she was a voracious fan. I, on the other hand, did not really believe in hope, if hope meant bridal gowns and a life without sports. So, after several summers of watching her daughters fidget at their post in the living room, our sun-toasted thighs sticking to the aqua-colored vinyl upholstery, my mother succumbed to the gringo reality that no suitor would be appearing outside our bedroom windows, serenading his longing with a mariachi backup, as young men did for my mother in her teen years in Tijuana.

I ruthlessly scavenged cupboards for traces of that mother—the one I had known in my childhood—and found only muted remnants in objects she had abandoned for decades. Had I had the heart, the red-and-black can of Calumet baking powder with the drawing of the Plains Indian chief on the label could have elicited the sound of her rolling pin slamming against the flour-dusted wooden slab, the picture of her brown arthritic knuckles diving into the white metallic black-rimmed bowl, whipping la manteca into perfect bolitas de harina. Had I the heart, I would have remembered tortillas the texture of fine paper, the hot mineral smell of the comal, fire against cast iron, the palpable moistening in the kitchen air as I entered it from winter outdoors play.

Possibly, as the objects that made up my mother's history no longer mattered to her, they meant less and less to me. For as I pried open the cookie-tin sewing canisters and small cloth-covered overnight suitcase that served as file cabinet at the base of a closet; as I fingered the fine golden hair de mi niñez stuffed inside a card-sized envelope, its seal broken; as I pilfered through endless piles of skirts and sweaters and pants that descended in size with the ascending age of my mother, it seemed since forever she had been so ill, since forever we had been losing what we understood as her "ser." I no longer knew any other mother than the broken one. In a different lifetime, she smelled of gardenias. That day, outside in her garden, the gardenias had already curled brown, gathering in a moldering blanket at the plant's base.

Maybe the house really didn't matter. Maybe neither three days nor three months would've returned me to that location of heart I knew as my mother's home. Still, on that late-autumn day, beneath the purple shadow of those languorous San Gabriel Mountains, I lit a sprig of cedar on an abalone shell. I raised an eagle feather to the rising smoke, passed it through the rooms of my mother's house, and prayed:

> Let this wing of memory greet my mother's spirits
> and send them flying home.
> Ya. Do not linger here.
> She will not be returning, I lie.

SIBANGNA

In 1977, as I stuffed my Volkswagen bug to its metal gills and headed north on 101, following in the highway wake of thousands of young people in pursuit of "liberation," I had no way of knowing that twenty-five years later, I would return to San Gabriel to uncover what was left there. Ostensibly in search of my mother's history, it was my own buried remains I sought. *But how do you dig up amnesia?*

Diggers. Digger Indians is the name the anthropologists first gave to the Indigenous peoples of California. A no-name people in their estimation, the Gabrieleños-Tongva of the Los Angeles basin were similarly denigrated, reduced to the image of broken nails scratching at an equally broken earth in search of supper. And yet this was exactly how I had felt scouring my mother's past for a sign of palpable memory, a sign that we were a people that predated suburban sprawl, mini-marts, and my family's en masse denial that we walked in cultural mourning.

The neighboring Mission grounds were the only testament to a history that predated Gold Rush California and all the gringo gold-digs to follow. I knew, even as a child, that it was the site of holy terror, where the memory of the Indian dead persisted if in nothing other than the mestizo bodies of my schoolmates, draped in plaid woolen Catholic school skirts and charcoal-gray trousers. We were immigrant "Mexican" and Native Californian—Tongva, Acjachemen, Chumash, Mohave, Yaqui, Shoshone, Cahuilla, Quechan, O'odham, and more—the descendants of those mission and desert Indians extending from as far away as San Xavier del Bac in southern Arizona to the coastal and inland regions throughout Southern California. Somehow, without saying so, the Indians buried beneath the tiled floor of that Old Mission Church were not strangers to me.

Four decades later, my sister and I enter the Mission Gardens. We stand beneath the same midday sun of our childhood past. I allow myself a moment's reprieve, to imagine an exchange between races as equitable as the coexistence of plant life in this jardín.

The garden displays what I love most about Mestizo California—that meeting of the Mediterranean and Native American landscapes: bougainvillea climbing over adobe walls; the muscled thrust of elder grapevines throwing arches of shade over broken cobblestone pathways; the petals of succulents brotando como flores; the desert memory of maguey and nopales with trunks as thick as torsos amid mounds of goldenrod and poppies; the scent of anise and yerba buena wafting lightly through a steady heat. Here the beauty of the native seems enlivened by the contact with the immigrant. I am as romantic as the tourist in this regard, longing to imagine a less brutal past. But spirit won't have it.

A grave marker states: "Antonio, First Indian Buried in This Cemetery, Oct. 20, 1778," shadowed by a life-size crucifix. Who *was* Antonio and what was his real name? What were the names of six thousand "neophytes" interned and interred within the quarter square mile of the San Gabriel Mission?

Inside the Old Mission Church, JoAnn is physically unable to enter the baptistery, in which resides the "same sterling silver baptismal shell" where "the first Indian child received the waters of everlasting life."

"I can't go in there," she says. And she can't.

I remember my sister-in-arms, the writer-activist Barbara Smith, telling me the same when, wandering down the streets of New Orleans toward the outskirts of town, she happened upon the former site of a slave auction block.

Spirit won't have it.

A decade from now, the first "Pope of the Americas" will come to Washington, D.C., and hold a canonization Mass for the California missions' founder, Junípero Serra. Pope Francis will not travel to California to bestow the honor, although Serra's body lies there entombed in the Carmel Mission. The pope's itinerary will not permit a parallel journey along El Camino Real, following in the dusty and sanguinary footsteps of the "saint's" sandals. The pope, a holy man, will not kneel down on those Indian burial grounds, kiss the earth, and ask forgiveness in the Roman Church's name.

For to walk that real road of history, he would encounter its original peoples, many of whom remember the mission system as bitterly as African Americans remember the plantation: as the site of slavery, subjugation, and ethnocide. And yet to this day, those sites paradoxically still matter to Native Californians as physical markers of the unrecorded Indigenous histories known in their bones and in scarcely remembered songs. The lands still resonate with their bisabuelos' receding original tongues and with stories told by the old aunties.

Just down the road from la Misión de San Gabriel a tiled mural acknowledging the contributions of the Tongva Nation overlooks the same neighborhood park we used to frequent as children. In the kiddie playground where Elvira once bounced her grandchildren on the spring coils of pastel seals, a replica of a Tongva village now stands. Surrounded by native plants used for medicine, baskets, and clothing, the site recognizes a scarcely documented history that predates mission days and acknowledges Sibangna as the original name for the area. There a community of some one hundred and fifty people had once made home.

Two hundred years later, my family did the same.

I have no papers to prove that my family moved to San Gabriel in 1961 as an act of cultural reconciliation; but in recent years I have wondered over curious geographical coincidences. Lieutenant José Joaquín Moraga served as second-in-command to Juan Bautista de Anza, in his second expedition to Alta California by way of the De Anza Trail.

The route parallels my own family's journey of migration and, in particular, my own: from the birth site of the Moragas in Altar, Sonora, México, in the early 1800s, to the meeting and marriage of my maternal grandparents in Tucson at the turn of the nineteenth century, followed by a leap in time and circumstance to eventually land Elvira Moraga y su familia two blocks from la Misión de San Gabriel. A near generation later, I would move to the San Francisco Bay Area and, soon after, assume my mother's Mexican patronymic surname.

Decades ago, serving as tour guide on my parents' visit to the

Bay Area, I pointed out the gravestone of Lieutenant José Joaquín Moraga, embedded in the tiled floor of Mission Dolores in San Francisco. Touting her sudden claim to fame, by virtue of her shared surname with the lieutenant, my mother pronounces to my father, "And you thought you married just any ole Mexican."

My dad and I smile.

If there *is* reason to believe that the Moragas from which we descended are remote relations of Lieutenant José Joaquín, it would probably be through the lineage of his brother, José Ignacio, and of the Moragas who remained in or returned to Sonora after the De Anza expeditions in the late eighteenth century. My great-great-grandfather José Moraga was born in Sonora in 1832. That's as far back as we know for (almost) sure. It also, of course, says nothing of the history of matrilineal lines threaded through the tapestry of my ancestors.

Many Sonoran Moragas were military men and warriors—from as early as the missionization period through the Mexican-American War. They were distant relations who killed Apaches or relations who were Apaches themselves. There was a Chiricahua chief who carried the Moraga name, as well as Akimel O'odham (Pima) and Quechan (Yuma) and mestizo Moragas—men and women in Arizona who are recorded in eighteenth- and nineteenth-century historical annals and whose descendants walk the same deserts today.

Whatever the actual historical scenario, my mother's patrilineal ancestors—European, Native, Mestizo—at some point intermarried or had sexual unions (by force or agreement), resulting in the mixed-blood band of Arizona and California Mexican-Americans we are today. Whatever the scenario, after World War II, in gratitude for the safe return of her sons, my maternal grandmother traveled with the Tohono O'odham in peregrinación from San Xavier del Bac Mission to Santa Maria Magdalena Mission in the heart of the Sonoran Desert. Did Dolores share the O'odham bloodline? I don't know. Did their cultural roads cross, intersect, and blend? Yes. The mixing would continue into my own generation and well beyond it.

What la familia Moraga shares historically with multiple generations of Mexicans and MexicanAmericans is the denial of our Native origins. As mestizos, we swallowed the bitter Kool-Aid of colonization—first through the Spanish and then the gringo— that distanced us from the recognition of a living Indigenous presence in our histories, our families, and ourselves.

At times, I felt my mother's prejudice in this regard, a bias directed even at herself, which always translated into a hyperawareness of skin shade. Fingering through half-century-old family photos, my mother would point herself out—"la india flaquita"— she always the skinniest and the darkest one, pressed against sibling shoulders. A fact, I suspect, first noted by her Spanish-skinned mother.

"Mira, la indita."

It is Christmas Eve, 1992, a family gathering at Tío Manuel's home in Montebello. He and I encounter each other in the narrow hallway. I am waiting to use the bathroom. He is a big man and there is little room for us both, but in that small space he finds the space to speak to me with a certain confidence.

"We were the Indians that built the Mission," he says. "It was all our land, the entire San Gabriel Valley." It is a short conversation, the time it takes for the bathroom door to open again and allow me entrance. But I have never forgotten it. Somehow this information was passed down to my tío over a period of two hundred years. Some other "Mexicans" taught him to remember in spite of all the internalized and familial anti-"indio" prejudice to the contrary.

My tío Manuel was an uncle by marriage to my mother's sister Eva. But to us he was family for more than half a century, as are his children. They, my first cousins, carry (perhaps unbeknownst to them) that same Gabrieleño (Tongva) bloodline.

I've learned some stories told by the Tongva/Kizh about their forced displacement when México secularized the missions in the 1830s. I've learned that Native familias banished from the mission fled into hiding in the same San Gabriel Mountains to which I contemplated escape as a child. The adults were hunted down and executed en masse. Soon after, their children, undetected by the military, returned "home" and homeless to nearby villages. There they found protection among the Mexican familias who took them into their homes where they learned to hide their Indian identity in order to survive.

But who were these "Mexicans" who offered them hogar, if not Native and mestizos themselves: people who had mixed biologically and/or culturally with the Spanish and/or who were "indios" from neighboring tribes. How else might the Tongva children have blended if not for the fact that their protectors also looked (were) Native?

How far back do we need to go for the reclamation of ourselves?

In 1821, after about fifty years of direct Spanish colonial occupation in California, the citizens of the newly formed independent México may have become mestizo in culture, but with the exception of the Hispanic Californios, remained predominantly Native in ethnicity. A mere thirty years later, in 1850, California will win AngloAmerican statehood and the identifiable Native population will have been decimated by 90 percent.

It is always a political act when we are named and when we name ourselves. "Chicano/Xicano" emerged in the late 1960s as a movimiento of Indigenous and mestizo self-reclamation. Today many of those same activists and their familias have recovered themselves as Kumeyaay, Tongva/Kizh, Chumash, Esselen, Salinan, and Ohlone. I am a displaced mixed-blood Chicana, whose Native relations on my mother's side may land me somewhere in the deserts of Sonora and perhaps, and quite distantly, in the once paradisal lands of the Tongva. There is something to be found in those sites where memory calls us, in spite of the institutional amnesia force-fed to us for centuries. We return as refugees to that forgotten landscape which we somehow recognize as home.

It wasn't until the last years of her life that my mother admitted aloud what I already knew from the character of her mexicanismo, that as a mestiza she was also "Indian." I don't remember exactly how the subject of her ethnicity arose; I only remember how the words fell so easily from her lips, this time without shame.

Bueno, también soy india.

Without tribal name or entitlement, and just as Alzheimer's was beginning to traverse the map of my mother's brain, the geography of that remembrance returned to her. It was not a grand statement, but it was grand to me. After a near century of denial, in the same way she had responded to her fifty-five-year marriage, my mother was simply done with the pretense.

REUNION

Maybe in this land of forgetfulness, my mother found a befitting place to forget.

On el Día de la Virgen de Guadalupe (December 12) in 2003, my mother is released from Della Martin Center after a stay of nearly six weeks. She is immediately placed in Expressions, the memory-impaired wing of Prestige, inhabited by those same shoe-shuffling elders in bunny suits from whom I had tried to shield her just a few months earlier. Now they would become her neighbors. A five-minute drive from my sister's home in Yorba Linda, the residence also held a Prestige single apartment waiting for my father, once he recovered from his hip replacement surgery.

Like most of Orange County, Yorba Linda is a city cemented in amnesia where sprawling malls, one-stop shopping centers, and "fifty-five and better" condominium developments encroach upon the few remaining citrus groves and Japanese-owned strawberry fields along the surrounding hillsides. My tío Eddie remembered the twenty-four-hour gym on Yorba Linda Boulevard as the packinghouse where his older sister Victoria worked, stuffing oranges into wooden crates in the 1930s.

Although we had made every effort to surround my mother with objects of meaning from her San Gabriel home—family photos and statues of saints and altar keepsakes—she seldom responded to them in her new environment. Instead, she inserted old meanings into new people and things. The wide carpeted corridor, with its walls decorated in 1940s memorabilia—AngloAmerican images of big-band dancehalls and World War II soldiers' homecomings—became her home hallway lined with family photographs. She occupied her day entering and exiting other people's rooms, fixing, folding, cleaning, emptying trash cans, doing activities not unlike those tasks she had performed in her own home all day long.

One day my sister, unable to find our mother in the common spaces nor in her room, found her in a male resident's room, helping him put on a sock. JoAnn was convinced that she had simply exchanged this man in her mind for our father, on whom she had waited hand and, in this case literally, foot for over fifty years. It seemed that the *physical* activity was what mattered to our mother's shrinking brain; and that her body be allowed to reenact behavior it had performed for her entire life. The actual context for the activities was no longer of any consequence.

My father had been in a nursing facility recuperating from his hip surgery, and more than a month had transpired since my parents had last seen each other. On the morning of his move into Prestige, I escort my father over to the memory-impaired wing for the reunion. I punch in the entry code, hear the latch release, and push open the heavy wooden door into the canned heat of Expressions.

The motionless quiet is what hits you first. As if the air itself holds its breath, waiting not for death exactly, but for the predestined unfolding of events. Ambulances are a regular occurrence, as they are on the other side of the coded door. But here, on *this* side of the dented coin that is dementia, the ambulance seems to be greeted with a dreaded hopefulness by the residents. They lift their faces up to watch the action. *Perhaps this time it is my time to die.*

That day when I search for my mother, we find her in the dormitory-style room she shares with another female inmate. The roommate is tucked inside her covers, unable to find the strength to rise during the day. My mother pretty much ignores her or refers to her with a kind of uninterested condescension. I am grateful for the privacy that the roommate's illness provides my parents, who are being unceremoniously reunited behind the closed door of this sleeping quarter.

My father is reserved, nervous. "Honey . . . ?" he ventures. She looks up from whatever task she has busied herself with. "Vera . . . ?" He goes to her, wraps his arms awkwardly around her, bringing the small bones of her shoulders into the wall of his chest. She responds, and I notice my father visibly sigh in relief. They embrace for a few brief moments. Then suddenly she pulls away from him, her face full of intention and indifference at once.

"I did the best I could," she says, and walks away.

In this reunion after more than a month of separation, my mother pronounced the end of their relationship. Sure, she would continue to see her husband, who would daily come to fetch her from Expressions. Balanced by a new combination of psychotropic drug therapies, there would be whole months before them in which my parents did not fight. But no fight also meant no Vera to reconcile either the last years of torment or the decades of embitterment that preceded them. In that statement, "I did the best

I could"—the last wholly relational sentence she would address directly to my father—my mother absolved herself of their embattled past.

She was, in effect, done.

The next night, upon my return to Oakland, I sleep against Celia's back and openly let the tears fall. At 4 a.m., I am up again, sadder than ever. "My mother is dying" is all I can think to say. "Brace yourself," Celia tells me. But there is nothing to support the broken limb of promised death. We learn to walk, at times crippled by its truth, as our own faces grow aged from the worry over who, when, how, how much longer . . . ?

"She's had a long life, eighty-nine years," I say with feigned confidence to anyone who asks, as if I were ready to let her go. And I was, surely, every time I saw her walk about the corridor of the dementia unit disoriented and anxious, carrying a lonely confusion about which room in this place of no locks and no exit was really hers; whose clothes, which bathroom, and where was the toilet? *Is the toilet the sofa you ask me to sit in?* She drops her pants, confused.

I am Elvira's daughter who awakens in the middle of the night and prays that it is her mother's death to which she has awakened.

Who prays to have this not-dying over with, once and for all.

POR COSTUMBRE

anuary 1, 2004. Oakland.

    I write on this first morning of the year that isn't a beginning at all, but a deep place of returning inward to the work of winter thought. The rain reminds me of this, a deep drenching of sorrow, running in rivulets into the leaf-clogged gutters of this gray-cloaked city.

    Still, I am happy just to be here. Because there is rain and the gray bay beneath it. There is the Rose Parade on TV, and my heart lightens when I see the National Band of Mexico from Puebla, playing an unrecognizable brassy number, march across the screen.

    Celia laughs when I tell her, "I love marching bands." I reminisce about my own trumpet-playing football-field-marching youth.

    "There's so much I don't know about you, querida," she says. We both like the idea of this fifty-one-year-old revelation of my "MexicanAmerican girlhood," as we refer to it.

———

On New Year's Eve, we had refused cliché in our marking of the year's end. The cold kept us indoors; there was no movie, no dinner out as planned. The kids had been sent off to other familia for the night. We lit the candles on the dining room table and sat down to a meal that seemed just enough: winter vegetables, a piece of meat, salad. I found the remaining bottle of red wine, given to us at Christmas. I poured myself a glass.

And true to custom, we look at each other. And I can tell behind Celia's eyes, which mirror mine, we are almost embarrassed by how contentas, in fact, we are just at the moment.

Custom requires a fire and we light one. I toss in a bit of prayer tobacco and realize I'm grateful for the heartache of the closing year. Somehow. Somehow, there is a kindness in it.

After dinner and another glass of wine, my mind conjures the scenario of my making love to Celia, how her eyelids drop when my touch excites, how she moves inside herself for me to find her, waiting.

We kiss and the mutuality stuns for a second. But to have sex is to push at something the moment resists; to consider friction and rising energy and orgasm is to interrupt the delicate balance of desirous quiet we have achieved this evening.

So we do not make love, but bring pillows and blankets onto the floor before the fire and talk and do not talk and hold each other until I find I have drifted off to sleep on her shouldered breast. We pull out the sofa bed, the fire dying down, turn off the lights from the Christmas tree, and fall asleep.

The quiet is not interrupted until the sudden rumble of firecrackers explodes into the fog outside our sala window. We stir.

"I think it's midnight," I say. And return to sleep.

EXPRESSIONS

"Prime-time Elvira" is how I thought of it. In February, my mother is administered memantine, believed to retard some of the gravest symptoms of Alzheimer's for a short period of time. In the months ahead, she comes to repossess aspects of her old self. This was, in a way, a last hurrah for my parents. My father could show my mother off to the residents and the Latina staff, whom she charmed with her effortless bilingualism, petite figure, enduring good looks, and doting affection.

During those months of drug-induced reprieve, my mother walked around like she owned the joint. In Elvira's mind, Latina staff became her nieces; and the meals served in the common dining area, a restaurant. Once a week she went to the residence beauty salon, where the stylist arranged her thinning scalp of returned-to-Indian straight hair into pseudo-jazz-age bobs she would never have tolerated were she in her right mind.

By springtime my mother had recovered her pre-hallucinatory state, with one unexpected difference: her outbursts subsided to periodic ruptures of high irritation, but never rage. She now recognized my father as her husband of fifty-plus years, but could not fully grasp why, at the end of each day, he went off to his room in the assisted-living side of the residence and she to hers, behind a door with a code she had not deciphered. She spoke complete and expressive, if not always coherent, sentences. She was in good humor much of the time. She even gained weight, from seventy-two pounds when she was first hospitalized to eighty, which looked good on her.

On one visit, I find my tío Eddie, sitting with my mother out in the Prestige courtyard. He holds his elder sister's hand with the confidence of a lover. She is fragile but quite "present." The next day, Rafa takes his grandma out to this same square, surrounded by manicured hedges and blooming plantitas. He gently tosses the plastic ball back and forth to her, she making a circle with her arms the way small children do. She catches it and smiles, and Rafa throws the ball back to her with the patient tenderness of a grandparent.

In the months ahead, there were occasional lapses, her mental health sometimes compromised by the relentless pain of osteoarthritis and the regular reappearance of blood clots in her legs. Since my mother's first foray into dementia care, my sister and I had been struggling to determine what degree of intervention we wanted from the medical establishment regarding our mother's physical condition. There were good days and bad. And each time any of her family members punched in that entry code to Expressions, we could not deny the visceral anxiety we felt, not knowing which woman would be there to greet us (or not) on the other side of that wooden door.

One day, anticipating my mother to be completely dispirited after a long bout of listlessness and exhaustion, I find her utterly present. Another slight change in her medications had returned her capacity for small pleasures. That day it was a bowl of soup, with a ring of crackers around it. She slurps the teaspoon of carrots, chicken chunks, and floating noodles into her mouth. Her hand does not shake as she finds the cup of coffee pleasantly bitter and warm.

James has come for a visit. And she sits among her three chattering children and quiet husband for a few good hours, fully awake and listening. At one point, my brother leans toward our mother to say something. She pulls away and looks at JoAnn and me. "Who's this?" she asks.

James's face flushes. We all just chalk it up to Alzheimer's, swallow the moment, and move on, for our mother had returned to us for just a bit longer. Somehow those few hours of conscious awareness in this vibrant being sitting next to us, enjoying the simplest of pleasures, eclipsed all the struggle that preceded it. This remained the ongoing mystery of Alzheimer's: what combination of a good night's rest, good breakfast, and good drug balance would bring our mother back to us, if only for a few hours.

Outside of those fleeting moments of reconnection, I would often have to press myself to recall my mother's laughter—the personality of Elvira—in her pre-dementia life. At best, I caught faint glimpses of her, like sudden Polaroid snapshots: my mother in a scalloped bib apron and red lipstick, flyswatter in hand, flailing at the swarm of flies hovering at the back screen door just before the guests arrived; my mother with outstretched arms in a thin summer housecoat, chanting, "Ay, mi angelito, mi hediondo apestoso," to my baby boy as he races up her driveway on sturdy toddler legs.

One spring day, after months of being cloistered, Elvira was so animated when she greeted her that JoAnn decided to take our mother out to a nearby Mexican restaurant. Midway through the meal, JoAnn put her on the cell phone to me. This was one of the things I missed most in relation to my mom, the ability to simply pick up the phone and talk to her.

"Cherríe? This is your mother. Cherríe?"

She had reached my answering machine. I hear the telltale hoarseness of her vocal cords through the gravelly recording, but her voice also possesses a youthful lightheartedness, her manner casual, relaxed, even as she searches for the words. She waits for my response, doesn't realize it's a recording.

"Mi'ja . . . ?"

Since she gets no reply, she hands the phone back to JoAnn.

I overhear my mother dismiss the project: "It's not that much of a thing."

My sister prods her: "Tell her you love her, Mom."

My mom complies. "I love you, mi'jita. Cherríe?" She pauses, hoping to hear my voice. "I love you, mi'jita. Please call me. I like to talk . . . about you. Come over," she insists, as if she has a whole house of her own in which to host me. "Come over at least for a little while, okay? I've been waiting for you to come."

And then the next line breaks me:

"Everything that I eat, I think, I say, my little girl . . ." and then I can't make out the rest, but I know the rest because I cannot remember one meal that I ever shared with my mother where she did not refer to which of her children or grandchildren were missing at the table—my brother, my sister, my nieces and nephews.

For my mother, meals were the site of familia. Her capacity to feed us was her capacity to mother us. So even when we were not present, she ate with the awareness of a place reserved for us at her table. La madre dadivosa had returned, if only for the length of a cell phone connection in which she used more words than I had heard from her in the past year.

I was not an orphan after all. Not yet.

SOME PLACE NOT HOME

During the stolen hours of my visits alone with my mother, I often worried how we would pass the time. In the ensuing months, she would lose most of her verbal language. On the best of days, she was reduced to a few rehearsed phrases of two or three words:

"It's a shame . . ."

"Mira, mi'ja . . ."

"You never know . . ."

"Cuidado con . . ."

"Tengo ha . . ." And she would gesture bringing food to her mouth.

I didn't doubt that my mother's stories still resided within her. I could often see the impulse rise up from inside her. It was so organic to my mother, the urge to contar, chismear, comentar, avisar, but the words no longer followed. She would struggle to draw her faithful listener in, pressing my forearm lightly, pointing with her eyes identical to the way I remembered my abuelita doing in the last years before her death at ninety-six. Theirs was a wry humor, an uncanny sense of irony, expressed in the raising of an eyebrow, the fallen corner of a mouth, a shrug of the shoulders. Celia often commented on how much my mother could say without words.

It is spring break and I have brought our family of four down from Oakland for a visit. We are in the activities room of Prestige. Celia and my mother watch our children, Camerina and Rafael, play pool, knocking the balls around the table. Rafa has the advantage over Camie, having spent long hours at the table during our regular visits to Yorba Linda. He's feeling at the top of his game.

I see my mom tug at Celia's wrist to get her attention. She points to Camie with her eyebrows, as Camie's newly acquired length and rounding adolescent hips, which mirror Celia's, lean across the table for a pocket shot. Elvira's milky graying eyes scan that body approvingly. She nods, with a kind of licentious arch to her eyebrows, and casts her eyes back to Celia. "Tiene un cuerpo bonito," I hear my mother say without words. The gesture claims a kind of a personal ownership, by all our abuelitas, of that emergent tribe of Mexican young women that follow. Celia nods in agreement, smiling.

Later, my mother and I will sit together in the quiet living room of the dementia unit. A gas flame creates the illusion of a real fire in the fake fireplace, logs stacked in a perfect zigzag arrangement. The day before, I had shared with JoAnn my worry over how to pass the time with our wordless mother. She had suggested magazines. "She likes to look at the pictures," she said, "especially of beautiful things . . . flowers, gardens, bridesmaids."

I grab one lying on the coffee table. It was a home-and-garden type, which I'm sure my sister had already shown my mother, and I am suddenly thankful for that small amnesia. The magazine yields anew dozens of pictures to which my mother can nod approvingly or frown at in displeasure. I turn the page and we land on the picture of a house whose rustic kitchen opens to a garden in full bloom. She points at the picture with enthusiasm; and then suddenly frowning, she indicates with her head the room in which we sit and the nearby kitchen area. There, elders are planted, some playing cards with attendants, others slumped in their wheelchairs in a nodding half sleep.

"No." She shakes her head. "Estoy cansada," her eyes plead to me. And then I get it. The picture is of home, a home she longs for. "This is not it." That many words she could say of this place of half-dead americanos and a stove that sits cold during the day. She wanted me to take her home.

"Sí, Mamá," I say, "real soon," wanting to believe that I would one day steal her away and bring her home to me. *Where the stove will stay warm all day long*, I promise to myself. Moments later, she would cognitively forget this conversation; of that I could be sure, but the spirit does not forget.

In the eighteen months my mother would spend at Expressions, her need for home was evident in all that she did. Her daily rituals mirrored what she had been accustomed to doing most of her life, from providing small tendernesses for other residents (patting the hand de una pobrecita) to cleaning crumbs from a tablecloth or rearranging shoes at the foot of a closet. Home had always provided my mother with a sense of purpose and sure-footedness in a slippery world. Bereft of her home, my mother improvised. Through pure invention, she created as much home as she could in her daily life.

There were whole weeks in which she repeatedly and secretively escorted JoAnn and me, at different intervals, to a large mantel-like furniture piece situated at the end of the Expressions corridor. She would motion for us to come closer and would wordlessly open one of the drawers containing a mauve dinner napkin she must have taken from the kitchen. Lifting the napkin, she would indicate the space beneath it as if to say that this was where those things of value would be found; that should something happen to her, this was where we would find what she had left for us.

The drawer was empty, except for a few clean tissues, but the gesture was pregnant with meaning. We remained her confidantes, the gesture told us; and she was still our mother-provider, our protector. "Por si acaso . . ."

"In case something should happen to you." I finish the sentence for her. She nods.

Expressions. Maybe the naming of these elder facilities was not as commercially intended as I had suspected, for my mother's wordless *expressions* eloquently articulated a complex web of emotion and body memory she carried inside her.

I recall this especially on those days when we would return our mother to the dementia unit after a day's excursion—maybe to the hot dog stand down the road or a few hours sitting outside under the shaded canopy of my sister's patio. There was no evading the sense that she was being deposited like a package whose contents could be collected and returned. She no doubt felt the same as I caught the sigh of disappointment falling out of her when I pushed open the door to the pleasantly upholstered front room.

For a long time, we would quickly steer her away from the door in the effort to ease the transition and to bar her from any sudden move to escape. But what was worse is that she eventually made no such move. She merely turned her narrow sweatered shoulders away from us (there was no real goodbye) and headed quietly down the hallway in the direction of some place *not* home. She had already forgotten the meaning of that spontaneous sigh and had moved on.

On such days, when the heavy keyless door locked behind us, JoAnn and I swallowed hard, full buckets of tears. I visualized the galvanized metal ones, like the work buckets that held soapy water on the Saturday chore days of my childhood; like the tub in which I had once bathed my mother when prefabricated showers no longer suited her. It was just turning spring in San Gabriel and Alzheimer's was a distant denied thought. Unashamed before her daughter, naked, she stepped in as delicate-toed as a heron.

NOW AND ZEN

When I finally came to accept the fact of my mother's Alzheimer's, it had put language to the loss of connection I had been experiencing from her for so long. Of course, one initially responds, *Not my mother.* At first, I had felt betrayed by the diagnosis; that Elvira would be denied a death with dignity. What I didn't know at the time was that the illness would come to illuminate my mother's spirit life, the ephemeral and the constant, in ways that the sleep of our mundane existence does not allow.

My mother's Alzheimer's offered its witnesses a slow reconciliation with our beloved's dying—the departure of the ego, of personality, of memory itself. *When I can no longer remember my name . . .* At some point, this final forgetting would happen to each and every one of us. I could only hope that in death, we are finally relieved of mattering so; not to our survivors, but to ourselves.

As Elvira's illness progressed, I began to experience her as my personal Zen teacher, observing her live her life in the perennial present. But her *body* continued to hold fast to the past. My father cried at the kindness of my mother's gesture of instinctively tucking in the back of his shirttail. Did her body remember, although the heart had forgotten the gesture's meaning? In the timelessness of my mother's remaining months at Expressions, we watched her degenerate before our eyes. She became noticeably less present, did not respond to my touch the same way she had; she remembered no one's name on her own. We were grateful that she could at least still recognize her husband, her daughters, her many relations.

Spirit relatives now surrounded her. I watched them call her attention, her head turning away as if listening to a nearby conversation. They drew her in more compellingly than the middle-aged daughters who comforted her, the youth (her grandchildren and their mates) who visited, hopeful and kind. My niece, Erin, said it best: "She isn't holding on to me any longer." There was a sad freedom in the release.

What I was witnessing in my mother and had registered intuitively is confirmed in science. If she lasted long enough, she would return to infancy. Some days she barely managed the skills of a two- or three-year-old. She could no longer dress herself. There was the day in which she placed excrement, like a child playing tea, on the plates of her sister residents. No one knew where she got it. "She's been stashing it places," the attendants suspected. Everyone, even the other elders, knew not to eat it. But none of her lady friends looked at her askance, for they were all children now.

With the celebration of my mother's ninetieth birthday on the fifth of November 2004, Elvira had already spent a full year behind locked doors. I don't remember one word from her that night, certainly not a full sentence. We sat in a small private dining room at the residence. Helium balloons were tied to the chairs circling the long table. My mother sported a plastic party hat, bowler-shaped and bright pink, with a band also dotted with party balloons printed in primary colors.

In one photo of the event, my mother profiles the same Yaqui nose of her mother at ninety. It shadows the length of her face. The bowler tipped forward, she looks the part of an aging Charlie Chaplin, sad in that same melancholy way of the clown, powdered cheeks and red-lipped.

But like the clown, just beneath the surface of her comic antics, in the beat between joke and laughter, my mother's pretense falls. In the span of an hour and a half she was completely spent. Barely poking at her meal, she smiled for photographers: first with her three children, then with her husband, then with her sister and elder nieces, then just the menfolk, then just the womenfolk, then with the grandson, then finally her face collapsed into itself.

"She's tired," my sister said. "Let's take her back," which meant to her usual spot in Expressions on the La-Z-Boy in front of the TV she never watched, where she would fitfully fall into sleep.

An hour afterwards, the attendant would take her to her room to put on her flannel pajamas and, if the night went well, she would manage to get my mother to fall asleep in the twin bed with the comforter that was too heavy for her bone-thin legs and arms. Elvira would try to lift the blanket with the side of her thigh but the effort made her tired, weak, and sleepless. Forcing herself out of the bed, she would wander the halls until dawn, when she would again fall into the La-Z-Boy and sleep until breakfast.

This was my mother's life now, and as alien as it seemed to her daughters, there were whole days in which JoAnn and I concurred that she was sometimes happier there in her imagined world of household duties, caring for others, picking up the napkins they dropped and dumping the small metal trash cans of other people's bathrooms, than in the enforced world of social relations.

After the "party," I return home to Oakland. Something had

shifted for me during my last visit. I scan a photo I had taken of Elvira at another family gathering perhaps a year before. The portrait bears no trace of my mother's anxious heart. Her eyebrows slightly arched, the expression is whimsical and forthright at once. She remains resolute, as fixed as the sculpted stone her aged face had come to resemble. I print out the photograph, find a frame for it and the courage to put it on my ancestor altar surrounded by my honored dead. The gesture, intuitively prompted, told me what I had begun to think of my mother: that she was daily becoming one of them.

WHEN THEY LOSE THEIR MARBLES

These are the gifts we daughter-lovers
offer to one another.
See our open hands.
You hold your medicine—paintbrush and peyote.
I, the writings my claw-hand scratches
against the broken pavement of my desire.

Through the obsidian mirror of death, I saw myself stripped of the illusion of my separateness from the suffering of others. Celia's eldest son, the troubled Maceo, nearing thirty, had returned to enter and disrupt our lives with a brooding disquiet. In him, I recognized the reflection of my own desperate attempts to control the women and children around me. He, with no other leverage than the volume of his voice, the threat of his fist, the guilt we women feel for the anguish of our sons.

Inside the body of my own fears, I knew myself to be equally abusive. I observed my feeble attempts to arrange my home and family life—those troublesome beings who are my loved ones—compulsively posting kids' pickup and delivery schedules, checking homework compliance like a prison guard, picking up small collections of lint from the rug as neurotically as I had as a child. Each day I told myself (and often Celia) that I was done fighting, worrying; desperately trying to ward off the worst-case scenarios of failing high school grades and unplanned pregnancies; of fast-food- and computer-game-addicted grandsons; of middle school truancy as a lifestyle prediction for my adopted familia.

I knew, peering into the mirror-face of death, that I could no more control the adult lives of Celia's children (nor how they managed their own children) than stop the progress of my mother's disease. At times, Celia and I would sit at the breakfast table, Camerina now a high schooler and Rafa off to middle school leaving their bowls sticky with drying avena, and we could do nothing more than lament the losses between us. We got up, washed and dried the bowls, and continued with our day.

I was sweeping outside when I heard the commotion from the downstairs porch. Maceo's voice was shaking and . . . livid.

"I don't know what you want!" he shouts.

"Want what?" Celia asks, stepping out onto the porch to better calm her son.

"When you die . . . I don't know what you want for a service!"

Earlier that day, Maceo had been helping Celia move some art items in a van, closely following her in his own car. He watched as she barely missed a head-on accident, swerving away just in time.

"You could've gotten killed!" he snaps.

I passed him on the porch on the pretext of putting away the broom. He glanced over at me bitterly. "You are nobody," his look told me, still unreconciled with his mother's lesbianism; blaming it for all the loss that he had suffered, convinced that it had relegated him to the fringes of the Native world.

Beneath the masquerade of all that masculinity, Maceo was sensitive enough to know that losing Celia was *everything*. In a later conversation, he repeated, "Just tell me what you want!" It was clear that Maceo didn't think that I had anything to say on the subject. Her death would be his to have. And I wondered—*Am I any different?* Don't *I* believe that I somehow hold the rights to my mother's passing? It occurred to me at that moment that Celia might prefer to offer herself over to her son in death than worry over the last rites/rights of our queer marriage. Oh, it *is* a marriage, but without contract. And as the gay politic of the day struggled for the legal right to marry, I tried to figure out, *What's blood got to do with it?*

Even before my mother's illness, Celia often lamented the horror of eldercare in this country. "When I lose my marbles," she'd joke, "just put a long rope around my waist and tie me to a tree out on a hillside somewhere," more than half meaning it. Somehow, I've never had a problem imagining her tethered to a great cottonwood in the sierras of her Ódami Durango homeland, where she would finally be allowed to return, if only for those extended moments of conciencia before the earth finally swallows us whole.

It was true that Maceo had often served as a thorn in our relationship, especially in his younger years. And yet he and his young daughter, Cetanzi—whom Celia parents in his stead—represent what Celia fundamentally understands as *pueblo*. I know I cannot interrupt this. As she does not stand in the wake of my ancestors, I cannot stand in the rising river of hers.

These are the words I do not say to my beloved's face but know them to be speechlessly true in my heart. These, my own queer marriage vows:

> *Through your son*
> *the one who gives you the deepest heartbreak,*
> *the one who into his thirties*
> *calls three and four times a day*
> *with a boy's ansias,*
> *who cannot quite yet*
> *figure out how to pay a bill*
> *not quite*
> *how to manage a full month's rent*
> *not quite*
> *how to get and keep a job*
> *whose heart and head*
> *ache from so much*
> *almost*
> *not quite*
> *and yet*
> *another daughter's*
> *promise is born.*
>
> *For this one girl-child,*
> *who remains with us,*
> *is somehow marked differently.*
> *She who, barely two*
> *walks about*
> *with great ancestral knowing.*
>
> *And the world stops spinning for a moment*
> *and the world makes sense for a moment*

that ancestors may in fact come back
to repair damages done.

And I watch your heartbreak turn to hope,
watch all other sentiment eclipsed
by this great knowing
that a pueblo can return
through the body of a broken boy
spitting out a grandmother spirit.

We came together through loss, Celia and I. She, an orphan at five, the daughter of a long litany of dead relations. I, the daughter of familial abundance. We came together with loss on the horizon; for it is not a matter of numbers but of memory.

I don't know how far back to go, except to say conciencia was born at my mother's breast; except to say as a child of god, I knew myself godless before I reached "the age of reason" in Catholic catechism terms; except to say that I am one among millions of delusional *Mexican*Americans, who has pretended we immigrated to (and were not born of) these lands; except to say that my mother danced with Rita Hayworth in the nightclubs of Tijuana in the 1930s, and it was downhill after that—not downhill easy, but sliding on your nalgas down the rocky descent of dying dreams.

In the last years of my mother's life, I resigned her to a place that was not home so that she could remain close to my father, instead of her lesbian daughter, four hundred miles away. Now I wonder. I wonder if it was the right thing to do when blood matters, when blood required me to bring her home to die.

PART IV

How can I tell you this? . . . That this stub of . . . pencil that moves across the page of paper is not real, either, and that the truth lies on the other side of even these words.

—*Four Souls,* LOUISE ERDRICH

THE WISDOM OF DOLPHINS

May 29, 2005.

At my mother's hospital bedside, I watch her dream in a drug-induced sleep/half sleep. I tell myself, Good, she is resting. *Don't know if it's so; don't know if the drugs help or hurt or if they snatch from her whatever conciencia endures. She sleeps openmouthed, sucking in the motionless hospital air. Her lungs are strong. Blood transfusion. IV drip for hydration. Busted hip repaired with plate and screws. I don't know.*

On Memorial Day weekend, wandering, as always, through the corridor of Expressions, my mother falls and fractures her hip. After that there would be no more birthday parties, no more trips to the nearby hot dog stand or the taco joint down the road, no more afternoons spent before the fake fireplace of Expressions, no more postponement of inevitable questions and irreconcilable answers.

The night before her surgery, JoAnn and I had sat with our mother in her hospital room. Fully rested from being forced to stay in bed, she was suddenly lucid and in good humor. Given her alertness, I ventured to tell her the truth: that she had fallen and broken her hip and that the doctors intended to fix it. Her lucidity was so remarkable that I also found myself saying that there was a risk that she might not come out of the surgery. She had earned this: to be told the whole truth, to have the chance to die "awake," is how I thought of it. "Nunca se sabe," I counsel, as the doctor had counseled us. This was the kind of language my mother understood best, where we offer up our fate to a universe we cannot control. *You never know. Si dios quiere . . . if it is God's will.*

"Entiendes, Mamá?" I asked, and she nodded yes, that she understood. But more than this, she knew, as JoAnn and I also knew, that this was really her deathbed farewell. For on that day my mother was fully coherent and she spent it embracing a long line of relatives who each got a chance (without admitting it) to say goodbye. Lifting my hips up onto the edge of the bed, I take her hand in mine, and drink in the etched beauty of her face. Her childlike expression is so utterly aware, a pure earnestness inside those liquid ash-colored eyes. She completely entrusts herself to me and to my sister. There is nothing more to lose.

We replay for her all the gifts she had given us as our mother, as a sister, an auntie, and abuelita: her good counsel, her generous heart, her tireless labor for us as a familia. I thought of the Tibetan Buddhists' prayer, "May I not die confused." And that is really all we want for our beloveds and for ourselves, to not drown finally in a pool of fear, regret, and uncertainty.

Without saying so, JoAnn and I vainly hoped that our mother would not survive the surgery. She looked good, everybody said . . . and happy. It *was* a good day to die. But she didn't die and we don't get to write the scripts, the happy endings, nor the perfect deathbed despedidas. That night, on the eve of my mother's surgery, was the last time Elvira would ever be as present to us again. The doctor had warned, "It is often the beginning of the end. Once they break their hip, they don't usually return to their former selves."

After her surgery, my mother was moved to Brighton Gardens, a nursing facility just down the Imperial Highway from Expressions. As the surgeon predicted, we witnessed in our mother a sudden, accelerated decline. Her exterior world was very small now. She was moved from bed to wheelchair and back again. Her family came and held her hand as she muttered to us and to herself, rehearsed phrases from the distant memory of another life.

She slipped in and out of dreams.

Questions I had rejected throughout my mother's illness returned to torment me.

To what degree is consciousness determined by the capacities of our brain? Where might her consciousness reside independent of her diminishing brain? In her present state, what might her transition unto death be like?

I knew, in truth, that these were spirit questions, even as I consulted science for confirmation. For, to look at Elvira, to *really* look, her interiority seemed to deepen by the day. She was speaking to the other side now. She seemed to not only remember but was able to foresee a future of otherworldly relations, unencumbered by the contraction of her brain and physical surroundings. There was no denying it. My mother's *facultad* was growing, but in this final stage of her life, it grew away from us.

Would I now only come to know her in my dreams?

◉

I am at a seaport. I walk along its boardwalk, a kind of pier extending into the water.

The slatted wooden walls of the buildings and plank boards are painted in Cape Cod gray and white. I am to go down through a hole in the floorboards, which leads into the ocean waters.

I sense that my mother is there and that my descent is as if to meet her, join her in her slow dying, or perhaps she was already dead in the dream. I don't recall. But I do go down through the hole and into the water without hesitation to be rejoined with my mother.

Suddenly a gray-blue dolphin approaches and wraps itself around me. I feel its smooth rubbery texture engulfing me around my waist and at first I am afraid of being strangled, squeezed to death by the strength of its hold on me.

But then I relax. I give in.

And this is the most pleasure I can remember,
to swim in the embrace of the dolphin.
In the embrace of life in death.

SOFT SPOTS

We were all such a long way from home.

When I arrived at Brighton Gardens that late July morning, I had been away from my mother for about a month. My son and I had just returned from Arizona and we landed in Southern California dusty, and I, broken with fatigue. It had been a hard road trip taken with Celia, who was fighting a relentless flu, along with teen-angst-ridden Camie and a recently "adopted" nephew.

Nephew had come to us via Celia's son Maceo, who had homesteaded with the boy's mother for a few years. Maceo was now gone, and we were left to respond to the boy in some way. It had been a kind of unspoken contract, after all, the promise of fatherhood from Maceo, something we two lesbians in our fifties could never fulfill for this boy. Throughout the trip, Nephew made every effort to show us how at twelve years old he was already a man, and needed little from us besides the price of a meal.

Throughout the too-long week away in the Sonoran Desert,

the site of my ancestral origins, I kept suffering the question of "home," and whether I was truly up to the task of this queer and makeshift familia, reconstructed from broken promises and spurned hopes.

And then suddenly on the first day of our return to California, I find "home" slipping away in an Orange County nursing facility. My mother's recovery from hip surgery had continued to be fitful and laborious, she falling into regular bouts of illness, rising irritation, and mounting depression. The physical therapy was each day leaving her more and more spent. And although my father was adamant about keeping my mother out of the wheelchair, my sister wondered if it was not the kinder solution.

When my father and I arrived at Brighton Gardens for that morning visit, the head nurse stopped us at the door. Vera's vital signs were dangerously low, she told us. She was dehydrated and needed to go to the hospital right away. It was a perfunctory recommendation, which we had previously responded to affirmatively each time our mother's vital signs dropped. Since her first hospitalization at Della Martin, Elvira had endured several short hospitalizations for blood clots and heart issues that would, each time, throw her into a state of panicked disorientation where nursing staff would have to restrain her physically. Moving her from her everyday surroundings often felt cruel, unfair, and unnecessary.

After the hip surgery, JoAnn and I decided that we would no longer passively accept such recommendations. Wasn't this the exact situation we had been preparing for for some time? "As little invasiveness as possible"; we had repeated those words over and over again, to ourselves and to her caretakers. On the other side of those words, nothing prepared us to make such choices—to determine for our mother the quality (maybe even the day) of her death. But these were the choices we were required to make when natural deaths were seldom proffered to our elders.

"Let me see her," I say.

When we enter my mother's room, the shades are drawn against the intensity of the summer morning sun. In the muted light, my mother is a small hill of blanketed gray. I go to her, put my hand to her forehead. It is cool, too cool. She appears to be sleeping.

I exit to get my sister on the cell phone. She steps out of a work meeting to answer the call. We confer with the nursing staff, and they with their administrators.

"What would the hospital do for her?" I ask.

"Administer antibiotics, a chest X-ray, provide oxygen and an IV for hydration."

"Can all this be done here?"

"Yes," the nurses respond.

"Then she is not to be moved," I say with full authority, doubting my every word.

Within an hour after the hydration and some antibiotics, a small dose of energy has returned to my mother. She is surprisingly better. I even manage to feed her a half cup of Ensure. I step out of the room for a moment to speak with the nurse. When I return, no more than ten minutes later, my mother is alert and animated; she seems to have forgotten the trauma of her near-death an hour earlier, when the slightly built Filipina nurse struggled to insert an IV as I steadied my mother's arm.

Now it is as if I enter the room for the first time. She exclaims, "Cherríe!" and greets me in full recognition of who I am. I go to her, embrace her anew. She had not said my name in forever, but that day, unprompted, she greets me as *me*.

By the time my sister gets to Brighton Gardens, bringing my son with her, Elvira is already exhausted and, after a short visit, falls back asleep. Minutes later, her primary physician arrives and, after taking one look at her, asks . . .

"Would you like hospice care for your mother?"

Observing Elvira, the muted physical presence she assumed in a matter of moments, it was in many ways such a benign question, a mere affirmation of what her daughters, her husband, the nursing staff, and the doctor could already witness, that Elvira was slowly yielding to death. There was no urgency to the doctor's inquiry. Hospice simply meant that she would stay on at Brighton Gardens, but without any further invasive procedures. Certainly, she didn't mean that our mother would go anytime soon, we told ourselves as the doctor spoke to us. It was merely a respectful gesture in the direction of the natural death we had sought for our mother. Our mutual yes emerged effortlessly—a quick glance between my sister and me, a look over to our father, who seemed confused but in agreement.

There is a small silence in the curtained half room after the physician leaves. The meaning of our decision begins to settle. Was my mother privy to this conversation where her loved ones wordlessly measured respect against betrayal, perseverance against hopelessness, regret against denial? *Have we merely grown too tired?* We ask this for all of us, including our mother.

Suddenly, without knocking, the physical therapist enters to shatter all hope. Clipboard in hand, she tactlessly announces there will be no more therapy sessions for our mother. Disturbed by her intrusion, JoAnn absently signs a form. And then it hits our father, as the therapist exits in a blur of efficiency.

"Does this mean Vera will never dance again?" Joseph still believed that his wife would return to him and put his two reconstructed hips to good use.

We had just said yes to hospice, yes to readying our mother for death. Ten minutes later, my father hears, *My wife will never dance again.* And somehow this one fact breaks him down right there in my mom's sickroom/deathbed. This floors him and us, too, because we thought he knew how sick she was. We thought he knew she had been dying for so long.

Elvira's eyes are closed, lips slightly parted. She breathes steadily and my father and sister, after a few hours' vigil, slip out to return to the business of their day. Rafa and I stay on to watch my mother, his Grama, move in and out of sleep. As if in a waking dream, her mouth moves with utterances I can't decipher, her hands whipping the air in the drama of some unknown story.

Rafael knows she is going, probably more than I. He composes a poem on the spot. She is "talking to the dead," he announces, no doubt in *his* voice. Then, exhausted, his abuelita drifts off into almost-sleep; for it is not quite sleep, but another place of being.

She is being called. I feel it, the pull on her from the other side, but I do not allow myself to recognize this, not in my body. It is too simple, too ordinary, too subtle; this shift from one world to the next. The room is animated with spirit; there is no mistaking it, but we are programmed in this culture not to believe what we feel. We deny and argue against this deeper knowing. We defer. Had not the physician said, "It could be weeks or months or even years from now?" Had my mother not just eaten from my hand?

Had she not just called my name in the gesture of goodbye? That was the truer question. Ignoring it, my son and I kiss her forehead and walk out to leave her alone to her journeying.

Let me tell you a story, a story of a family in shock and mourning.

Watch the family go to the county fair. We fly above the treetops, our legs dangling like expectant skiers over the blacktop flatlands (once orange groves), neon reds and yellows spinning beneath us; blues blasting from one corner, punk rock from another.

We do not celebrate; we mourn. We play "pretend" that Elvira is *not* dying.

The big-band orchestra plays, too, under the fairground tent, and I suavely sneak up on my father, who sits with a half-eaten leg of chicken on the paper plate in front of him. I ask him to dance. We are not ashamed to dance right there on the asphalt pathway because this is after all the last dance, the dance reserved for my mother, which my father does with a holy vengeance, spinning me around in Vera's stead. I can't miss a beat and don't because dancing was the one thing they really enjoyed doing together, the one thing they shared without ambivalence.

His grip is like nothing I ever felt from him before; so tight, it is almost violent. He swings me wide and tethered to him. His eyes are wild with three glasses of red wine in his gut and a forged public smile. The dance is a rough-and-tumble toss and turn, which I keep up with, so that it *looks* smooth and partnered. But Daddy's dancing to his own tune, I think, dancing against the brutal rupture of the one thing that meant joy in his life. Dancing with his wife.

After the dance, we leave Joseph to nurse a cup of coffee, and we walk about the fairgrounds. I love my sister enough to know that she needed to pretend tonight: she, with her grown son who escorts my son about the fair with an elder brother's tenderness. At one stop, I watch Rafa, with spindly spider legs, scale a fabricated mountain wall; I watch him dump cash into the pockets of the money-grabber three-balls-for-five-bucks barkers. My son is a gambler, weighing the odds: the remaining crumpled bills in his pocket and the accuracy of his free throws against the coveted prize of those giant stuffed basketballs.

Brian came of age today, too, I think. On his first day as a

teacher for special ed kids, one pisses on the floor in defiance, saying, "F you, you mother-F-er," as my nephew puts it. And I know
Brian got broken just a little bit today, learning that the strength
of his character alone would not ease these troubled kids. He
enters the adult world of powerlessness.

And I sigh, forgiving us all our soft spots.

Five hours later at three o'clock the next morning, I am pulled out
of bed by the force of Elvira's passing. I don't know it then, that this
is what draws me up and out of bed and into the backyard of
my sister's house. But as I stand barefoot beneath the fog-shrouded
moon, the same moon whose light filters through the half-open
slats of my mother's room just a few miles away, my heart bears
witness to the change.

I am suddenly at once bereft of a god and full of a prayer's urgency. I cry out to that moon, "Show me a sign."

It is an orphan's prayer, I know.

"Tell me we made the right decision."

And my respuesta comes at seven o'clock that morning, when,
rising to go to the bathroom, I hear through the thin walls of my
sister's bedroom the twenty-month-imagined phone call.

SOLA CON LOS DIOSES

When the earth element is gone, you cannot move anymore. When the water element goes, your lips are dry.
When the fire element goes, you start losing heat. When
the air element goes, you stop breathing, and your heart
stops beating.

—GEHLEK RIMPOCHE

She was alone with her gods when she left this world. Maybe
that is what shatters the daughter's heart, knowing that
even the greatest love is eclipsed by the power of the spirits'
summons to the dying.

I don't know what I had hoped; perhaps that I would witness
my mother's last exhale, believing this was the closest I could get to
her spirit. As faithful sentry, I would be the last to pass her on to
relatives on the other side. I imagined myself that important; that
her death would not be impartial.

But death *is* impartial.

Twenty minutes after that 7 a.m. call, my sister and I arrive at
Brighton Gardens. We wait to inform my father; we wait to know
what we feel. We avert the compassionate looks of the attending
staff who step aside as we wind our way to the last room in the
corridor. The room that contains our mother's deathbed. When

we enter the room, I am relieved to see that she is the same hill of gray we witnessed the day before, except that a carefully folded towel props up her chin. The transformation is so fundamental and so subtle at once; for there was no mistaking that our mother had not yet left the room, that she was everywhere *outside* that body, as if her spirit had simply slipped out from that vessel, that bowl of bones and guts and elegance placed upon the bed, and had drifted into the air above us.

I tell my sister, *She's here, JoAnn.*

I had been praying to my mother's *spirit* for years, since the onset of her illness, and as the energy that was *she* permeated the air around us, I knew that this was the same *she* I had prayed to. It was the same energy moving through and out of that brain and body that had contained her for nearly ninety-one years, but never completely.

Now she was alone con sus dioses. I held her hand *after* death. *After* death, I took her sculpted face and skull into my palm. With water drawn from the sacred springs of Mount Shasta, JoAnn and I washed the skeletal grace of her legs and arms, her distended belly (always the site of discontent), her olive-graying skin that lay like oilcloth along her delicate bones.

JoAnn had been the one, among others, to find the Mount Shasta spring as the Winnemem chief had directed. She and a search party of friends had left the base camp of our ceremony to listen for the water lying clandestine beneath the June snows. That had been two years prior, and as we gathered the few items from JoAnn's house in preparation for sending our dead mother home, JoAnn had remembered the jar of water.

Oh, I touched my mother *after* the breath had left her body, my hand moving across the carve of cheekbone, the noble arch of her forehead, her parched mouth. She was so present that it startled me to brush past her lips and encounter that vacant site of breathlessness. Had I thought she would still be breathing some-how? This body, whose *living* air had fallen upon my head and face as intimately as my own breath, had emptied itself once and for all. Without our witness, her last breath of life had spilled from her being into the air around us.

My mother died before she'd have to start another day. Per-haps she had been that exhausted. Maybe, as others have testified, the dying cannot depart in the presence of their most beloved survivors. Maybe the day before, as my mother appeared to sleep, she had listened with her heart's ear to our words. Maybe she had heard us let her go. "It's okay, Mamá," we said with our decision to accept hospice.

An hour later, I drive to my father's place at Prestige. I do not rehearse the lines in advance, as I wend my way, quick-stepping through the puzzle of corridors to his studio apartment. I want to simply let come what comes. I enter without knocking.

When I tell my father, the first words out of his mouth are: "It's been so hard for me." He, too, is relieved. There is no deny-ing it: the purgatory of Alzheimer's has been a great trial for him. And yet I am disturbed that his *first* words are about himself.

On that morning of my mother's passing, my sister and I and my father, and my tío Eddie and auntie Lola, keep vigil over her body, until the funeral people come to retrieve it. We pray the Ro-sary. We whisper cariños to her, grasping what memory we can in the knuckled repose of her hands. Every half hour or so, my tío steps out for a cigarette. He returns shrouded in Lucky Strike smoke, his shoulders a bit more bent by the lucklessness of death.

"She's gone home," he says, contemplating the blanketed fig-ure of his almost-mother, which is the best thing anyone can think to say.

COYOTE CROSSING

*I*t's when you least expect it. El Coyote leaps out of the snarl of blackberry bush and flashes across the roadway. You nearly hit him, but then he gets away with it, meat between his teeth. And you wonder if you imagined the memory of his appearance.

The amazing efficacy of patriarchy is that it is a covert operation. It is entre nos, just between us—man and woman, sister and brother, father and daughter, queer and not so queer. It takes place behind closed doors, inside la hacienda and back there in the slave quarters. It is so seamlessly woven into the fiber of our lives that to pull at that dangling thread of inequity is to rip open an entire life.

My mother's portrait, which had occupied my ancestor altar for many months, now sits upon a small wooden table at the foot of the white marbled altar. A lone veladora casts a warm light upon her face. It is the only site of Mexicanism amid this Catholic Church's minimalist sacred suburban design.

The funeral proceeds routinely under the deceptive haze of Orange County brightness. The sun, a whitewash, is a silent conspirator in my mother's erasure. There are spirits lurking, unreconciled in their namelessness. I know this by a palpable absence; by the sullenness of my blood relations. We have not made peace with this polite passing de la familia. My mother, truly its last matriarch, is now dead, and the tribe goes with her.

I place my attention on the portrait at the base of the altar. Only through that elder face that looks back at me, dark and foreign amid such deadening summertime brilliance, am I able to find the courage to rise from my place next to my sister in the front pew and approach the sunlit stairs to the pulpit. The face of the aged monsignor, also a marbled white, stands at the periphery of my fixed stare. My mother's hardening flesh, upon her death, stirs more vividly in my imagination than this pale priest, my brother's confessor and my mother's adversary. She had not trusted the man with whom James had often broken bread at a table to which my mother was not welcome. My hard leather soles tap across the altar floor. I step up to the pulpit.

This is the moment in which I had imagined I would eulogize my mother with words that emerged from the fluidity of our connection. *Even as my life took on directions she could not portend, she'd never stood in my way.* Stupid words. Stupid words would not do. Arrogantly, I had imagined myself greater than the speechlessness of my sorrow.

My eyes scan the gathering of suited pale professionals and middle-aged matrons in summer jersey. *Who* are *these people? My siblings' friends? Business associates?* I cannot find the old faces. *Where are the old ones? Was I mistaken? Have they all vanished with my mother's passing?* I look down at my notes. They look back at me, utterly useless.

I begin and try to speak the impossible, of what my mother

meant to me: that I had prayed to her as ancestor before her death; that I would miss her smell, the feel of her rough fingers stroking the hair from my forehead; that from her Mexicanism I had learned every value that is worth something to me to this day. But each word I utter is swallowed up by a ravenous hollowness. *Where are the old ones?*

"I want to honor my brother," I continue, "for finally saying last night at the Rosary vigil words my mother had waited a lifetime to hear." I taste the lie in the word *honor* as it drops from my mouth. We both knew his words came too late. Saying so was my small revenge. But I speak beyond volition; my words, captive hummingbird wings fluttering furiously inside my throat. I go on to acknowledge my sister's "fierce warriorship" and my father's "unfailing presence"—small rhetorical gestures at truth. The words push and stumble past my lips through stammered sentences and long pauses as I desperately try to construct my next line. I glance over at JoAnn in the front pew. Her steady gaze remains fixed on me, as my brother seethes next to her, his face red with building rage. My father is pressed between the two of them, numbed and deafened by his own private sadness. I search my vacant mind for one true thing to say for my mother and then it erupts:

"She was not requited in this life." And already I know I have said too much. I feel my brother, a stranglehold on my throat.

I press on.

"She was so grand. We could neither grasp nor hold all that she desired." And then I add, "Even my father knew this." He half nods in agreement, only a sad acceptance on his face. My eyes land upon my tía Eva, a cousin or two, among the sea of white faces. Frozen in their own grief, I read no response from them.

◉

At the Rosary vigil the night before, the spirit of the gathering had felt so different, at least in the beginning. The altar Celia had arranged for Elvira was ablaze with ánima—flores, lighted velas, white blossoms floating in a glass bowl of water. There were pictures of Elvira surrounded by familia at the pivotal moments of her nine decades. Mexican ballads played from speakers over the quiet hum of relatives saludando uno al otro con abrazotes y lágrimas.

Si Dios me quita la vida antes que a ti . . .

My mother's body, tastefully attired, as my sister had arranged, was presented in an open cherrywood casket. *She looks good*, I think, the way I remembered her before her illness. I notice a slight smudge of lipstick on her cheek. I let it go, appreciating the lack of perfection in it. The casket sits upstage to the right of the altar Celia has built. I call my sister and brother over to it and we light the candles in a gesture of reunion.

"Mira, Mamá, we are all here together," I say aloud, but it feels forced, performed.

Soon after, I see James's wife and their four adult children entering the mortuary chapel. They are strangers who move in single file through the assembled. There is a murmuring among the relatives, as the five scoot into an empty pew. *Is that them? Is that James's family?* The aunties and elder cousins lean against one another, whispering, since most of them have never seen any of James's children, now well into adulthood. As I am my mother's host, I go over to greet my brother's family. There is no "I'm sorry for your loss" from Aileen, only "Where's James?"

In the years of my mother's illness, I remember seeing Aileen visit her only one time at Expressions and very briefly. She watches my brother embrace our very ill mother and I see Aileen's eyes well with tears. I do not know if she cries over the waning of my mother or my brother's impending loss, or perhaps a moment's regret over having been so distant. I do not care. She cries for *something* that is of our family. But there is no sign of such feeling at the Rosary.

After my brother has collected his wife and moved her into the front row, he rises to give the eulogy. His eloquence stuns and disconcerts, for his speech is a love treatise to our mother. He honors her, the history in her hands, her hardworking ways, her devotion to Saint Anthony, her dignity of bearing.

My relations are confounded.

Had he felt that way, they would murmur later, *why had he never told her so? Why had he spent a lifetime separated from her? Why had he allowed her to suffer his absence?*

As James continues speaking, the energy in the chapel shifts. I become physically unsettled, and Celia grabs my hand. Through tears, I watch my mother's portrait blur behind the small lake of candlelight. She is just nineteen in the Tijuana studio photograph, but with the contained look of a woman of thirty. James reinscribes my parents' half-century union as a benevolent agreement signed solely by our father, where he had generously "released the reins" of their marriage to his wife's considerable will. Cowardice and self-interest had nothing to do with it. Suddenly the containment begins to crumble. My brother's voice in the foreground, I watch the expression of her portrait change into one of entrenched fury.

Is she angry with me? I worry, my heart pounding. Have I betrayed her by doubting my brother's words? I am a fifty-two-year-old woman, yet these are the thoughts of a little girl.

Celia hands me a bottle of water. I try to steady my breath and the palpitations in my chest. I grow dizzy. *Have I come all this way to have my mother leave me like this?* I am staring not only at my mother's portrait, but at the portrait of my own prison: my absolute impotence as a Mexican woman under the ultimate authority of my brother's words. They render me guilty and shamed.

Is this not also what my mother suffered? The self-blame, the lie of her father's integrity, her elder brother's authority, her mother's complicity in this legacy of male neglect? The same neglect proffered Elvira by her only son and a benign but weak-hearted husband?

Suddenly, there is the sound of glass breaking but James continues without interruption. Celia quietly rises, goes to check on the altar, yet there is no sign of disturbance.

Later, after the other testimonials and a slide show of our mother's near-century-long life, I gradually recover myself. La familia begins to slowly exit. I cross over to the casket to observe one last time my mother's reposing body when I notice the shattered glass of a large mortuary candle that hangs red and broken just above Elvira's head. Celia spots it at the same moment.

"Her spirit is so strong, Cherríe," she says.

When I returned to my sister's home after the Rosary, I stayed up all night drafting a eulogy for my mother's funeral that refused the pen. It was as if James had stolen my words and I was left speechless. I scratched at my pages of notes, trying to unravel the intricate knot of what her life meant to all of us—my mother's surviving siblings, our cousins, nephews, nieces, the grandchildren and great-grandchildren; but all I could arrive at was: my mother, the family matriarch, has died, carrying a great llanto of discontent inside her.

The next morning, I stood at that Roman Catholic pulpit, where the representatives of the god I had renounced upon my womanhood were authorized to speak. So I had no real authority to speak, I knew, more certainly at that moment than at any juncture in my life. I knew that regardless of how JoAnn and I had foolishly tried to ensure we would have the last word on our mother's life, I could not speak, not fully.

I could not say that I had not believed my mother's protestations, her pose for strangers in an Anglo world. I could not say that I had been the recipient of different messages; that she had told me discordant things, desires she could not live up to, but that perhaps were once tasted in the urban freedom of 1930s Tijuana.

I could not say that in my heart, I understood her body like a lover, because the wants of women are not foreign to me; and that I was not afraid to hold her as a daughter of that knowing. I could not profess what I knew to be so; that my mother was a woman of unyielding poderes that would not be suppressed.

The possession of the mestiza mother by the white patriarchs. This is what I felt for Elvira, looking out upon that funeral congregation. This censored knowing tied my tongue, muted the underground stirrings of insurgent ancestors. But standing at that pulpit, a memory spirit broke through me, and my eulogy became a rebellion.

ROUNDHOUSE

I walk about our Oakland home como una sonámbula, unable to place the *missing* in any one spot. The lingering absence of my mother is evident in each and every shadowy corner and creaking floorboard. It permeates the very air of the house. But I am spent of spirit; only a numbing sadness remains.

Seeing this, Celia slips out of the house and, hours later, returns with a small piece of furniture to serve as an altar for my mother's passing. It would provide a location for my loss. "For a full year," she says. But as Celia and I carry the wooden cabinet up the two flights of brick stairs, Celia misses a step and falls on the second-floor landing, breaking her leg.

One week later, she is back in the hospital with a pulmonary embolism.

She had awoken that morning with her back racked with pain. At first, we thought it was a muscle spasm from a long and strenuous week of carrying around the weight of her broken leg. Finally, she asked a family friend, a young massage therapist, to come over to help dislodge the disabling knots in her back. After hours of work, when the pain became unbearable, Celia called me downstairs to get her eagle feather and tobacco. Invoking the Winnemem spirit of Grandma Flora, who had thirty years before healed a traumatized and ruptured Celia, she holds the feather and instructs Alma and me in her own healing.

As Alma's fingers follow a huge marble of pain through a network of roadblocks, I blow the cigar's smoke into every site of stoppage. Together, the three of us travel with that knot of excruciating pain up and through Celia's long torso until at last she feels the blockage burst, spilling a battery of tiny pellets into her chest.

Later that night, Celia's discomfort persisted and we ended up in the emergency room. After many hours of testing, the embolism was discovered, but, as the physician explained, none of the blood clots was big enough to block the artery to her heart. That one large marble of pain, which Celia had felt travel up her back, had been a blood clot headed for her heart. This near-death incursion, so close to my mother's death, hit us both hard. It was as if an undercurrent of messages was trying to reach us, but I would not heed them.

I remember.

At my mother's burial.

The monsignor had handed the two brass crucifixes that sat upon Elvira's casket to my sister and me. I felt the wet of the monsignor's breath in my ear as he leaned into me and whispered words I could not discern. But a chill ran through me. And I was left disturbed, unsettled.

I remember.

The early morning following the funeral. The call that takes only a few minutes. JoAnn comes into the bedroom to tell me James has demanded to see her.

"I don't want her," meaning me, "to come. If you bring her, I'll leave."

Within a half hour, they are seated outside at a nearby Starbucks. He has already stopped the promised check for the trio of musicians that had played for our mother's burial. Now he has only one question:

"Did you know what Cherríe was going to say in her eulogy?"

JoAnn quickly searches his heated face. She has been subpoenaed to appear and on this witness stand, she is allowed only a yes or no response. No is an indictment of her younger sister, isolates me as the sole culprit in what James perceives as a conspiracy against him. But she feels it, his seething indignation, and the truth is, JoAnn had not known.

"No," she responds.

After that, she is not allowed to speak and my brother spews out all the rage he holds toward me.

JoAnn described his anger as like nothing she had ever witnessed. "Like he was possessed," she said. "It was so ugly, Cherríe, the things he said about you."

She did not have to tell me. I had already read it on his face from the distance of the pulpit—felt the palpable sense of his hands around my throat.

That day over a Starbucks coffee, my brother had the where-withal to stay the hand of his grief-stricken anger, tossing in my sister as a buffer to bear the brunt of it.

"I felt my mom protecting me," JoAnn said, "like this great shield came up between us. I heard James's words, but I could not feel them. They couldn't get to me."

Perhaps this, too, was the deeper intention in the sequence of events: that my sister was able to feel our mother finally rise in her defense.

Once Celia was discharged from the hospital, I wrapped up the crucifix and sent it on to James. *This was intended for you*, I wrote. Then Celia and I, along with Rafa and Erin, jumped into the car and drove three hours north to Winnemem Wintu land. I had invited Erin to bring her pure love of her grandmother with us. And to bear witness.

We were to sit before the Winnemem fire in gratitude for Celia's life and to pray for healing. And for protection.

As Celia limps into the roundhouse on crutches, Chief Caleen, Grandma Flora's daughter, hardly acknowledges the "accident"; for it is not an accident, the chief concurred, when the synchronicity of events cannot be explained away by logic. Celia had taken the fall for me and they both knew she was strong enough to handle it.

For, although Celia sat with her leg in a cast propped up on a milk crate, staring at the roundhouse fire, *I* was the broken one. *I* was the one needing healing. *I* was the one whose grief spun like a filero splitting my already ruptured heart. Celia had merely stepped in the way of the blade in my defense.

When the Winnemem chief finally lays her hands on me, the root smoke enters me hungrily. I long to be devoured by it. But there is no mystery to this healing. I inhale and breathe out the diablitos that have occupied me for a lifetime. Or so I pray.

The fire in the center of the roundhouse smells of old oak, peach tree, and acorn-ground earth. We watch the fire for many hours. As we pray into the night, the charred branches take on the shape of serpents and wagging tongues. Crooked-limbed men split apart in the belly of the heat; their mocking mouths melt into ember before turning to silent gray ash.

"Go home and take care of your family," the chief tells me, after many hours with the fire. She means my woman and our tribe of kids. "You know how to do this. They need you."

This is not what I expect to hear. I came to be "healed," to be relieved of my burden. But she tells me to go back home and shoulder it again. My mother would've done the same; did the same with every loss she encountered.

"Look at your son," she goes on. She has smoked him with the root. I do, and his look is simply of the most profound and unequivocal compassion.

"He's afraid that you loved your mother so much, you'll have nothing left over to love him."

But loving him is easy, I think. *There is always so much left over for him, siempre.*

Loving my woman is harder. We are not blood relations, so we imagine we can choose. Our loving is bound by nothing more than the whimsical movement of the heart, the infidelity of circumstance. When does it get to be too much? Too many bills, too many kids adopted into one overtaxed heart? But the truth was that if I closed my eyes, inhaled the smoke of that burning prayer, and saw only with my heart, there was nothing to distinguish the loss of my mother from the prospect of the loss of this familia, forged by this fire and built with my bare hands in the grasp of Celia's.

Her spirit is so strong. I remember Celia's words at my mother's vigil, and I know. My broken state was not the result of an evil eye or the magic of malice. It was a mother spirit, before and after death, leading a daughter back to this place of return.

This woman's fireplace.

The Native Country of the heart.

FOR THE RECORD—AN EPILOGUE

Nine months after my mother's death, my sister, son, and I would pass by my parents' home in San Gabriel just to look at it; just to see if there was something left to be found there. We had in fact left an old emptied trunk, its lock busted, and a rusty blue wheelbarrow, which I had hoped to bring home with me when I next had the chance. The chance came more than two years after our dismantling of the house, when I had finally found the resolve to return.

As we make the U-turn across the four-lane Junipero Serra Drive to pull up in front of the house, we see an older, well-groomed gentleman, pressed khaki work pants and button-down shirt, rolling up a garden hose on the blacktop driveway of the house. The place looks the same, but nicer than during my parents' last years there, when gardeners tended toward mediocre maintenance without my mother's constant regañadas.

The elder holds the end of the hose and watches us with a frown of suspicion as we park and step out of the car. "He must be the owner's father," JoAnn says. JoAnn had followed the sale of the house and was gratified to learn that it had been purchased by a Latino couple. We had feared the house would merely be razed for the construction of yet another apartment complex.

We approach.

At first, as we try to explain who we are, the conversation is reserved and awkward. And then relief passes over the elder's face when, struggling with his English, JoAnn and I readily shift to Spanish.

He apologizes that our things had been discarded after so long when no one came to get them. *We* apologize that we were so delinquent and assure him of this several times. "No se preocupe, señor." But recovering the abandoned items turned out to be a mere pretext for the visit; for what this elder gentleman was to give us, guiding us through the grounds of what had once been our home, would matter so much more than any rusty wheelbarrow.

The day before, we had gone to my mother's grave site, a small plot of thick Bermuda grass, neighbored by thousands of other Spanish-surnamed gravestones. It was Mother's Day at the Resurrection Cemetery en las lomas de San Gabriel and las familias had brought coolers and lounge chairs and umbrellas in anticipation of the high-noon sun. Folks hung out, eating, praying, and weeding the grass around the graves; washing them down with rags and buckets of water. We, too, with my father and my mom's remaining brother and sister, prayed and sang and told stories about my mom, and it felt good for all of us. But something was missing. Elvira.

For it wasn't until the next day, when JoAnn, Rafael, and I were back in San Gabriel and stepped into that garden of seventy-five-year-old rosebush, blossoming camellia, bougainvillea, and poinsettia that my mother's spirit presented itself.

Standing beneath the canopy of century-old blossoming jacaranda, it came to me that we are as much of a place as we are of a people; that we return to places because our hands served as tender shovels in that earth; that those yellow-peach and cream-colored roses, that wild yerba buena, las verdolagas covering the earth like loosely woven cloth to catch the steady drop of rose petal and leaf, this was my mother's constant site of comfort. And this jardinero guardian angel was custodian to it—that small lot of land and my mother's memory.

How egotistical we are to believe that when someone dies, they leave their spirit with *people*. Yes, I carry my mother's DNA, but she left herself equally in that patch of earth, where she had always offered her best self. Without tombstone marking, without plaque, without store-bought flowers stuck into the mouths of cast-iron vases dug into the graveyard earth, this was her earthbound site of remembrance more than any cemetery.

It is a warm September afternoon and I am digging, digging through books on the "Gabrielinos," books on the mission system, books of my own scribblings of remembrance and regret. I search websites, library databases, sift through photographs of "Californios" and the first Native "Angelinos," the computer-screen facsimiles of Spanish land-grant maps, and some early baptismal records of the missions.

I land on one, which distinguishes itself in that it is the first recorded baptism of "un indio" en la Misión de San Gabriel. I examine it, line by line. On that same manuscript of calligraphic letters, I spot the name Moraga. I can barely make out the fading script, which reads "Bautizé solemna otra adulta como 40(?) años, Viuda [y?] su consorte gentil y madre de los niños . . ." The two children are named Joseph Joaquín Moraga and María [de?] la Luz Moraga. With a bit more research, I learn that *gentil* in colonial Spanish is defined as a "heathen (unbaptized) indio." The register notes the baptismal site as the nearby Tongva village of Juyuvit and is signed by Fray Junípero Serra in November 1778.

This matters to me somehow: the proximity of Serra's ethnocidal signature, my maternal family name, and the Indigenous words for places I once knew as home. It is my own personal record that testifies to a complex system of mixed-blood misnomered historical erasure.

To disappear into Mexicanism is not enough; to disappear into Latinidad is even less of who we are; to disappear into Anglo-America, our colonization is complete. We were not supposed to remember.

There is no religious justification for the Spanish mission system, which effected a genocidal practice of slavery, dislocation, disease, and rape against Native Californians, and laid the groundwork for the two centuries of Native obscurity that followed. There is only greed.

There is no justification for the betrayal of the promises of Mexican Independence against the Tongva, the Chumash, the Cahuilla . . . There is only greed.

Since the arrival of the gringo in the mid-nineteenth century, it is first and last greed that has whitewashed the entire history of Native California, even as it walks still in the bodies of its "Mexican" descendants.

There is no justification, but there is so much need for reckoning; for me and perhaps for Elvira, too. And in that reckoning, there is the need for return.

My mother left her self planted there in those rosebushes in the once Tongva village of Sibangna. That's it. It was she who brought our Moraga clan to San Gabriel and its surroundings in 1961.

I return through these pages.

SELECTED BIBLIOGRAPHY

Some books that mattered to me, along the way of this writing.

Anzaldúa, Gloria. *Borderlands/La Frontera: The New Mestiza*. San Francisco: Aunt Lute Books, 1987.

Caspary, Anita. *Witness to Integrity: The Crisis of the Immaculate Heart Community of California*. Collegeville, MN: Liturgical Press, 2003.

Cixous, Hélène. *Three Steps on the Ladder of Writing*. New York: Columbia University Press, 1993.

Cooney, Eleanor. *Death in Slow Motion: My Mother's Descent into Alzheimer's*. New York: HarperCollins, 2003.

De Hennezel, Marie. *Intimate Death—How the Dying Teach Us How to Live*. New York: Vintage Books, 1998.

Didion, Joan. *The Year of Magical Thinking*. New York: Knopf, 2005.

Erdrich, Louise. *Four Souls*. New York: HarperCollins, 2004.

Frank, L., and Kim Hogeland. *First Families: A Photographic History of California Indians*. Berkeley: Heyday Books, 2007.

Guerrero, Vladimir. *The Anza Trail and the Settling of California*. Berkeley: Heyday Books, 2006.

Gunn Allen, Paula. *Pocahontas—Medicine Woman, Spy, Entrepreneur, Diplomat*. San Francisco: HarperCollins, 2004.

Gutiérrez Baldoquín, Hilda. *Dharma, Color, and Culture: New Voices in Western Buddhism.* Berkeley: Parallax, 2004.

Hanh, Thich Nhat. *No Death, No Fear: Comforting Wisdom for Life.* New York: Riverhead Books, 2002.

Hogan, Linda. *The Woman Who Watches Over the World: A Native Memoir.* New York: W. W. Norton, 2001.

Kimball, Sandy. *Moraga's Pride: Rancho Laguna de los Palos Colorados.* Moraga, CA: Moraga Historical Society, 1987.

McCawley, William. *The First Angelinos: The Gabrielino Indians of Los Angeles.* Banning/Novato, CA: Maliki Museum/Ballena, 1996.

Moraga, Cherrie. *The Mathematics of Love.* World premiere at Brava Theater Center, San Francisco, CA, August 12, 2017. Directed by the playwright.

———. *Waiting in the Wings: Portrait of a Queer Motherhood.* Ithaca, NY: Firebrand, 1997.

Narby, Jeremy. *The Cosmic Serpent: DNA and the Origins of Knowledge.* New York: Putnam, 1998.

Rimpoche, Gehlek. *Good Life, Good Death.* New York: Riverhead Books, 2001.

Shenk, David. *The Forgetting. Alzheimer's: Portrait of an Epidemic.* New York: Doubleday, 2001.

Wallace, David Foster. *Infinite Jest.* New York: Little, Brown, 1996.

ACKNOWLEDGMENTS

Agradecimientos.

To my beloved of twenty-one years, Celia Herrera Rodríguez. She opened a road for me, gave me permission (as it were) to return to the old stories, to believe I had a right to return. She also, just plain and simple, loved me—when I was not easy, when there was never enough time to write, when reliving the moments in this memoir sometimes stole my heart. I thank our children—Camerina, Cetanzi, and Rafael—for the gift they gave me in parenting them, each at distinct junctures along our shared paths. I thank my son, Rafael, most for this—for the uninterrupted nature of that path and for his continued courage to speak his truth in the formidable face of my own limitations.

Deep gratitude to Stuart Bernstein, my literary representative, for his patience and humor, his editorial eloquence, his strength of character and purpose. He not only encouraged me along the road of writing *Native Country*, he believed in and defended me. I marvel at this pure blessing—to become trusted friends in this way.

Gracias to my elder primo, Carlos García, who still holds familial ground in Arizona, and who began his search for our raíces through the desert towns of Sonora long before the at-your-fingertips virtual searches of Ancestry.com. Gracias a David Gonzáles, who tracked me down via those same internet searches to uncover that his father and I have grandparents who were siblings. His research was enormously helpful.

I have been gifted the generous professionalism of the editorial, publishing, and marketing team at FSG, especially Jackson Howard, Stephen Weil, Rebecca Caine, and Jeff Seroy, as well as the insightful legal counsel of Mark Fowler. Thank you. I am indebted to executive editor Ileene Smith, who was first drawn to the intimacy of this mother-daughter story, which also drew me to Ileene. I was so heartened by her open admission of what she did *not* know of my cultural world three thousand miles from hers in New York City; for in that aperture of not knowing and knowing, we found a cross-cultural conversation that helped shape this book into authentic existence. Mil gracias.

Doy gracias to my literary comadres—Helena María Viramontes and María Herrera Sobek—upon whose sisterhood I've come to rely. I am beholden to my Yoruba practitioner homegirls in Oaktown—Arnita, Xochi, and Sauda—for their ceremonies and faithfulness to the ancestors that have sustained us all. Ashé. Gracias a mi amiga fiel and personal assistant, Elisa D. Huerta, for so many years of support, as I also thank mi querida Myrtha, por su confianza en mí. I bow to my ever-teacher, Alice Joanou, who taught me how to breathe again, and to Ryumon Sensei for our people of color sangha in the years surrounding my mother's passing.

I am also grateful to my creative writing students at Stanford and now at UC Santa Barbara whose collective desire to tell an honest truth continues to inspire my own. I thank the Hedgebrook writers community and Yaddo artists' residency for the writing time and all the universities and communities that have provided me entrance for the opportunity to present and grow my work.

Tlazocamati to La Red Xicana Indígena and Las Maestras Center for Xicana Indigenous Thought and Art Practice, whose political and philosophical existence as cultural activist organizations has helped me realize my aspiration to serve as a woman of my word.

I thank all my family members, living and ancestral, who occupied the unspoken world of this memoir, especially mi querida prima hermana Cynthia Moraga García, who bore witness to many of the tales told here. Gracias to my queer hijo/hija, Cathy Arellano, for her loyalty and love, and for the growing familia that she and Gina have offered me through my nieto, Amado. I thank my father, now ninety-five, for our precious time together and for the remembered stories of his past. I thank my brother because he is my brother. And finally, I thank my sister because JoAnn is, in a certain way, the instigator and receiver of this work as I pass it on to Chicanas/Latinas who share her story.

Y a mi mamá . . . bueno, todo el libro está escrito en agradecimiento a ella.

A Note About the Author

Cherríe Moraga is a writer and cultural activist whose work disrupts the dominant narratives of gender, race, sexuality, feminism, indigeneity, and literature in the United States. A cofounder of Kitchen Table: Women of Color Press, Moraga coedited the influential volume *This Bridge Called My Back: Writings by Radical Women of Color* (1981). In 2017, after twenty years as an Artist-in-Residence in Theater at Stanford University, Moraga was appointed a professor in the Department of English at the University of California, Santa Barbara, where, with her artistic partner Celia Herrera Rodríguez, she founded Las Maestras Center for Xicana Indigenous Thought and Art Practice. She is a recipient of a National Endowment for the Arts Theatre Playwriting Fellowship Award and a Rockefeller Fellowship for Literature.